Oliver Flügel-Martinsen
Critical Political Theory

X-Texts on Culture and Society

Editorial

The supposed "end of history" long ago revealed itself to be much more an end to certainties. More than ever, we are not only faced with the question of "Generation X". Beyond this kind of popular figures, academia is also challenged to make a contribution to a sophisticated analysis of the time. The series **X-TEXTS** takes on this task, and provides a forum for thinking *with and against time.* The essays gathered together here decipher our present moment, resisting simplifying formulas and oracles. They combine sensitive observations with incisive analysis, presenting both in a conveniently, readable form.

Oliver Flügel-Martinsen is professor of political theory and history of political thought at Universität Bielefeld. His main research fields are theories of the political, democratic theory, contemporary French philosophy and social theory, as well as Post-Marxist critical social theory.

Oliver Flügel-Martinsen

Critical Political Theory

Interrogating Contemporary Politics

Translated from German by Michael Thomas Taylor

[transcript]

We acknowledge support for the publication costs by the Open Access Publication Fund of Bielefeld University.

Bibliographic information published by the Deutsche Nationalbibliothek
The Deutsche Nationalbibliothek lists this publication in the Deutsche Nationalbibliografie; detailed bibliographic data are available online at https://dnb.dnb.de

transcript Verlag | Hermannstraße 26 | D-33602 Bielefeld | live@transcript-verlag.de

Cover design: Kordula Röckenhaus

https://doi.org/10.14361/9783839400043
Print-ISBN: 978-3-8376-5215-4 | PDF-ISBN: 978-3-8394-0004-3
ISSN of series: 2364-6616 | eISSN of series: 2747-3775

Contents

1. Introduction

In the preface to his *Elements of the Philosophy of Right*, written in 1820, Hegel lays out his understanding of philosophy: "As far as the individual is concerned," he notes, "each person is in any case *a child of his time*; thus, philosophy, too, is *its own time comprehended in thoughts*."[1] In making this claim, Hegel articulates a critical social and political philosophy of the present rooted, to an unprecedented degree in the history of ideas, in a sociological interrogation of society. Over the two centuries following Hegel's remark, the history of theory has indeed been repeatedly and profoundly shaped by attempts not only to take up this task but to deepen and enlarge its scope, moving its aims beyond the mere recognition of reality. Marx, whose critical social theory owes a crucial debt to Hegel's model, likewise made the analysis of the present one of his foremost concerns but always insisted that such an analysis must serve as both a preparation for, and prerequisite to, transforming the world. His famous eleventh thesis on Feuerbach—"The philosophers have only *interpreted* the world in its various ways; the point is to *change* it"[2]—captures this task while simultaneously offering a critique of philosophy, demanding that it realize its emancipatory potential.

Since then, the commitment to a critical analysis of the present, coupled with transformation realized through practice, has repeatedly shaped the relationship between theory and society. We see this dynamic across the many movements for social and political emancipation since Hegel and Marx: in the labor movement, in

---

1   Hegel, *Elements of the Philosophy of Right*, 21, emphasis in the original.
2   Marx, *Concerning Feuerbach*, 423, emphasis in the original.

campaigns for women's rights and civil rights, in student movements across the globe, and the many other such movements arising in their wake. Again and again, the impulse familiar from Marx pushes to the fore: the drive to actively shape social reality. And Marx himself, critically appropriating Hegel, conversely insisted that a necessary precondition for any meaningful attempt at change was an adequate understanding of the present. Marx understood that reality cannot be reshaped unless we recognize the changes that are ripe for action; otherwise, theoretical reflections will remain nothing but abstract, wishful thinking. As Marx writes: "It is not enough that thought should strive to realize itself; reality must itself strive towards thought."[3]

This is perhaps one reason why theory with a dual edge, of critique and emancipation, has lost much of its practical impact in today's world. Looking around, we see that in many places, reality seems to be moving in a very different direction—certainly not toward progressive ideas or their realization. Right-wing populist and nationalist politics, rooted in a semantics of exclusion, have become normalized in most Western democracies. In some of these countries, right-wing populists are already in power, relentlessly working to replace democratic institutions with those of a populist-authoritarian system. The language of democracy long served as a powerful tool in the struggles of social movements for liberation and equal rights. Now, however, right-wing populist parties and groups have seized upon it, using democratic rhetoric to justify exclusion and inequality. And wherever they gain access to political institutions—even more decisively so when they come to power—they translate these words into action.[4] Nationalism, chauvinism, racism, sexism—these appear to be the ideologies defining a new reality that demands our attention. Has the long heyday of theory pressing for emancipation and liberation truly come to an end, destined to be become an object of historical inquiry

---

3   Marx, *A Contribution to the Critique of Hegel's Philosophy of Right*, "Introduction," 252.

4   See Müller, *What Is Populism?*

and a relic of the past?[5] And if so, does this mean that a theoretical perspective seeking to interrogate contemporary politics has become obsolete—precisely because theory has proven powerless vis-à-vis a social reality that increasingly appears to make mockery of any attempts at emancipatory change?

In my view, this interpretation is too simplistic in crucial ways. For one, we cannot situate our theoretical perspective on the present within a straightforward narrative of historical progress—one that Hegel and Marx employed, through their philosophy of history, to legitimize their own theoretical projects, and that was later embraced, implicitly or explicitly, by social and political movements that saw themselves as leading history forward. Perhaps we can better grasp the reality of social and political struggles by understanding them as a complex and dynamic interplay of movements and countermovements, as suggested by Foucault's theory of discourse. From this perspective, the political discourse of our time cannot be reduced entirely to the disturbing and undeniably dangerous rise of right-wing populism. Again and again, and often in unexpected ways, counterdiscourses emerge—ones that not only shift the political agenda but also introduce a fundamentally different political stance. Some years ago, movements such as Fridays for Future, #MeToo, and Black Lives Matter channeled outrage, not into exclusionary hatred, but into an emancipatory struggle to shape the future. While right-wing movements reject global responsibility outright, framing it through nationalist resentments, these other movements have, from the outset, been transnational in many respects.[6]

Certainly, the time when theories from the social sciences and philosophy were widely expected to drive fundamental social transformation is long past. By now, such aspirations have largely been relegated to autobiographical recollections[7] and historiograph-

---

5   See Felsch, *The Summer of Theory*.

6   For a philosophical perspective on new protest movements, see von Redecker, *Revolution for Life*.

7   See Raulff, *Wiedersehen mit den Siebzigern*.

ical studies.[8] Still, even now under these changed circumstances, theory could serve an important function in a present shaped by the dynamic between discourses and counterdiscourses—provided that it embraces the task of critically interrogating the conditions of our time. What theory must not become, however, is a glorified voice of historical progress. The predominantly Eurocentric history of thought marked by ideals of progress has not only revealed that such a stance is outdated, as a cultural construct fundamentally shaped by imperialism, but also that it has always depended on erasing the victims of the very progress it champions.[9] Hegel could describe history as a "slaughter-bench"[10] and celebrate it all the same because he believed he could discern, within it, a forward movement in the consciousness of freedom and its social realization.[11] Walter Benjamin, by contrast, radically inverted this perspective in his *Theses on the Concept of History*: For him, the so-called history of progress appears, when seen looking back toward what has been, as nothing more than a "pile of debris."[12] In this light, Benjamin called for a conception of history that recognizes "the tradition of the oppressed" and acknowledges the "state of emergency, in which we live"[13]—a state that has by now become the norm.

As these reflections suggest, we would do well to learn how to think and act without the comforting but ultimately deceptive assurance of a theoretical framework allowing us to see ourselves as part of historical progress. But this immediately raises a pressing question: How, then, do we confront those tendencies that are today often labeled as "regressive"? What can we set against the resurging specters of nationalism—forces that have already once dragged us into disaster—if we abandon the defense of concepts such progress or civilization, now that we have come to recognize them as part of

---

8   See Felsch, *The Summer of Theory*.
9   See Allen, *The End of Progress*.
10   Hegel, *The Philosophy of History*, 35.
11   See Hegel, *Philosophy of History*, 33–34.
12   Benjamin, *On the Concept of History*, 392.
13   Benjamin, *On the Concept of History*, 392.

a history of domination shaped by a culture of imperialism?[14] Do we not find ourselves compelled to seek out new normative points of reference that can be used to articulate critiques of nationalism, right-wing populism, racism, homophobia, transphobia, and misogyny?

The core argument of what follows is that a skeptical, interrogative approach to political theory—and more broadly, to social and cultural theory—is particularly well suited for an incisive critique of the present that *also* offers powerful lessons for its realization in practice. Of course, strong objections have been raised against approaches that replace fixed truths with critical interrogation. Paul Boghossian, for example, has broadly categorized such perspectives under the label of constructivism and criticized them for fostering relativism.[15] Michael Hampe in turn takes aim at what he calls the left-wing of cultural studies, which he sees as having relied too heavily on deconstruction and skepticism toward truth. In his view, this has unwittingly enabled the rise of populism, leaving one powerless in the face of post-truth politics.[16] In the chapters that follow, I will nevertheless seek to show that it is precisely a skeptical, interrogative stance that allows us to challenge the exclusionary essentialisms which right-wing populist movements and parties so effectively deploy today.

For a project of this kind, which seeks to critically interrogate the present, neither of two dominant approaches will suffice. One focuses on justifying norms, as seen in much of today's normative political philosophy. This approach largely abstracts from the social and political world.[17] The other, common in empirical political sci-

---

14 On the use of terms such as "civilization" or "regression" to critically interrogate the present, see Nachtwey, "Decivilization: On Regressive Tendencies in Western Societies." On a critique of Eurocentrism that nevertheless seeks to uphold the concept of progress, see McCarthy, *Race, Empire, and the Idea of Human Development*.

15 See Boghossian, *Fear of Knowledge*.

16 Hampe, *Katerstimmung bei den pubertären Theoretikern*.

17 For a critique of this development in political philosophy, see Geuss, *Philosophy and Real Politics*. Axel Honneth makes a similar critique at the beginning of his study *Freedom's Right* (2014, originally published in 2011):

ence, is theoretically narrow and fixated on formulating empirically verifiable hypotheses. It often relies on economic theories of politics that presuppose the model of *homo oeconomicus*—one that even economists have increasingly come to question. I will argue that neither is adequate. Moreover, both are aligned in having abandoned the task of analyzing contemporary society through a social-theoretical lens on two fronts: in their conceptual foundations and in their disciplinary positioning.

In their *conceptual foundations*, these approaches neglect the exploration of social and political contexts for differing reasons. This becomes clear, for example, in their failure to address the formation of subject positions—one of the core questions of political theory. Analytically driven normative approaches in political philosophy assume moral subjects as a given, attributing to them free and equal rights. From this assumption, they then evaluate the justice or injustice, appropriateness or inappropriateness, of principles and norms. Economic approaches in empirical political science build their models on the highly questionable category of the *homo oeconomicus*. Rather than explaining anything, this concept itself requires explanation. A well-grounded critical interrogation of the present must instead ask how subjectivation occurs. This entails considering both its contextual conditions and the power structures that shape them. In their *disciplinary positioning*, furthermore, these approaches have resulted in negative consequences from the so-called professionalization of university philosophy and political science. Both fields, namely, have increasingly adopted research standards that emphasize specialization over broader inquiry. As a result, academic work has become overly focused on technical, niche questions. At the same time, publishing practices have shifted toward a fixation on peer-reviewed journal articles, which have scant public impact. More generalist approaches to thinking and publishing have, by contrast, become rare. Ultimately, then, the

---

"One of the major weaknesses of contemporary political philosophy is that it has been decoupled from an analysis of society, instead becoming fixated on purely normative principles." Honneth, *Freedom's Right*, 1.

retreat from a critical interrogation of the present is tied to both conceptual and institutional changes in troubling ways.[18]

Political theory is often accused of avoiding practical questions and instead focusing on abstract reflections about broader structures and fundamental principles. In this essay, however, I will argue that a certain approach to political theory—precisely when it considers broader contexts—is in fact particularly suited to critically and insightfully engaging with urgent practical issues. For a project of critical interrogation deeply concerned with practical relevance, we need a theoretical approach that avoids two pitfalls. On the one hand, it must not restrict itself within a rigid, scientistic framework. On the other, it must not become so abstract that it disengages from social processes and structures to focus only on justifying norms and principles. Before turning to specific critical analyses of the present, Chapter 2 will outline the idea of a critical political theory that can sustain such a project. This will introduce a theoretical and conceptual framework that, in my view, is well-equipped to guide critical interrogations of the present.[19] This chapter will also set the stage for the directions that the following analyses will take. The subsequent chapters will explore various aspects and themes within a critical interrogation of the present. The goal is not to provide a comprehensive assessment of our times. Instead, the focus will be on developing critical perspectives on key developments that pose serious challenges to the future of democratic and emancipatory politics. I will particularly emphasize scrutinizing how right-wing populists appropriate democratic language to advance agendas opposed to emancipation. Chapter 3 will revisit the critiques of skeptical approaches to theory mentioned in the introduction. It

18   Of course, there are always striking exceptions, coming from both established and younger scholars. Still, an unfortunate trend can be observed: The so-called professionalization of philosophy and the social sciences has led to a growing shift away from contemporary critical interrogations that adopt a broader, more generalist perspective.

19   For a comprehensive explanation of this type of theory, supported by its historical development in theory, see my discussion in Flügel-Martinsen, *Befragungen des Politischen*.

will argue that positions fundamentally skeptical of truth do not, as some claim, fuel populist post-truth politics. On the contrary, they provide the tools for a sharp critique of such politics—one that can also open up new possibilities for a radically democratic practice of interrogation. Chapter 4 will examine contemporary obstacles to an emancipatory politics of radical democracy. Specifically, it will analyze the link between the ongoing dominance of neoliberal politics—framed as a matter of necessity—and the rise of right-wing populist movements. The core argument is that we cannot fully grasp the political success of right-wing authoritarian parties and movements without understanding how neoliberal hegemony has made them possible in the first place. Chapter 5 will focus on the resurgence of essentialist exclusionary politics, a defining feature of right-wing authoritarian movements. These movements have—with alarming success—reintroduced such politics into mainstream political discourse in Western democracies. Finally, Chapter 6 will situate these political developments within the larger context of a world defined by borders. This discussion will address these issues in light of the often-ignored question of global injustice.

Together, these elements form a mosaic offering a critical inter-rogation in the sense I aim to develop here. As the chapters of this study will show, the value of political theory lies not only in articulat-ing such an analysis of the present but also in showing that we are not confined to this moment—that we have the ability to move beyond it. For a vision of radical democratic transformation to emerge, po-litical theory must not assume the role of guiding the way forward. Instead, it must take on the dual challenge of being both modest and ambitious: It must contribute to a critical political practice through an unwavering questioning and challenging of the status quo.

***

This book is an English translation of a completely revised and up-dated version of my essay *Kritik der Gegenwart*, originally published in German in 2021.[20] I would like to thank my wonderful translator Michael Thomas Taylor for his outstanding translation of my book manuscript and his very helpful advice on it. Many thanks also to Nunu Büllesbach, who helped me with literature sourcing and supported me during the publication process.

20   The German essay builds on earlier preliminary work, with significant portions—some slightly revised, others extensively reworked—incorporated into the text. These include, first, "Befragung, negative Kritik, Kontingenz"; second, "Postidentitäre Demokratie"; and third, "Zeit der Pandemie, Zeit der harten Wissenschaft? Furthermore, the first section of Chapter 6 includes a revised version of my contribution to the symposium on Andreas Cassee's study "Globale Bewegungsfreiheit," published in *Zeitschrift für philosophische Literatur* 2 (2017). See also Oliver Flügel-Martinsen, "Sind politische Grenzen eine moralische Frage?"

2. Critical Interrogation, Negative Critique, and Contingency: Outlining a Critical Theory of the Political

The notion and concept of critical theory, originally shaped by the Frankfurt School and those who have engaged with it, have long since developed beyond any single intellectual tradition or approach. In the following, as I examine the contours of a critical theory of the political, with the aim of sketching a political theory capable of providing a critical interrogation of the present, I always use the compound term "critical theory" in this broad, pluralistic sense. Such a conceptual pluralization is warranted, if only because numerous contemporary perspectives—whether distinct or combined—claim to be variants of critical theory. It would be entirely contrary to the spirit of critical theory itself to impose rigid classifications or exclusions based on traditional authority or orthodox self-definitions. In speaking of "critical theory"—which I thus distinguish from the (earlier) Frankfurt School—I refer not only to theories rooted in various generations and branches of this original group of thinkers but also to those informed by frameworks of poststructuralism, deconstruction, gender theory, postcolonialism, and post-Marxist thought, among others, as well as approaches that blend multiple influences. Nevertheless, this does not imply a purely nominalist understanding of critical theory, where anything labeled as such automatically qualifies as such. Despite their differences, these various strands of critical theory share a common trait—at least in broad terms: Critique involves a fundamental interrogation of existing orders, structures, and meanings, always situating them within a complex web of power relations. A central point of contention is how this interrogation should be carried out and what it presupposes. The spectrum of views is vast, with major disagreements over whether a materialist social theory is essential, whether social and cultural meaning systems should take precedence instead—or in addition—and if so, how exactly this should be conceptualized and implemented. Another key debate concerns whether critique requires justification or legitimation at all, or whether it should deliberately forgo both. Given the sheer complexity and breadth of these debates, it should come as no surprise that the following discussion will not attempt to map or categorize this discourse in its entirety. Instead, I will focus on demonstrating the usefulness of a specific conception of critique for developing a critical theory of politics and the political. While occasional references to other notions of critique may arise—perhaps even necessarily—a comprehensive review of the full theoretical landscape is beyond the scope of this discussion.

In this chapter, I will outline a critical theory of the political, drawing on recent debates about radical democracy. This theoretical perspective is less concerned with establishing normative foundations for critique and is instead guided by the logic of negative critique—one that interrogates existing semantic, epistemic, social, normative, and institutional orders, revealing their contingency in the process. At first glance, this form of critical theory may seem disconnected from the broader intellectual tradition of the Frankfurt School. But upon closer examination, surprising parallels emerge with the project of critical theory as developed in Adorno's writings. This is evident not only in its fundamental orientation toward negative critique but also in its deeply interdisciplinary approach, which bridges philosophical inquiry into critique with sociological analysis of how social order and subjectivity are constituted. Moreover, it understands the political as a fundamental mode of world-building, in which aesthetic dimensions of perception play a crucial role.

In what follows, I will attempt to systematically outline the contours of such a critical theory of the political.[1] To do so, I will focus on three key dimensions. First, I will show that a specific interpretation of the distinction between politics and the political opens up space for an interrogative critique—one that rigorously examines existing social orders and forms of subjectivity with an eye toward their potential for change. As will become clear, this interrogative critique leads to a broad claim of contingency, which ultimately reveals the lack of any essential foundation or grounding for social and political structures, or for subjectivity. This constitutes the social-theoretical ambition of such a theory of the political: By exposing contingency, it also highlights the mutability and transformability of subject forms and social orders, making the task of developing a social-scientific lens for a critical interrogation of present particularly urgent. I also want to emphasize that interrogative critique is a form of negative critique—one that does not depend on justifications or legitimations of normative reference points and therefore rejects the notion that critique must be obligated to justify its normative standards. This is precisely where striking parallels emerge with Adorno's approach to critical social theory.[2] Yet, as will be discussed in Chapter 3, the fact that interrogative critique is a form of negative critique does not mean that it cannot contribute crucial insights to an emancipatory understanding of democracy. This will be explored in greater depth in the discussion of the relationship between skepticism about truth and radical democracy. On the contrary, a critical theory of the political—one that highlights both the constitution and potential subversion of existing orders and forms of subjectivity—paves the way, ex negativo, for a theory of radical democracy.

1   Of course, this approach entails certain necessary simplifications. For a more detailed discussion of this theoretical framework and its historical background, see Flügel-Martinsen, *Befragungen des Politischen*. Many of the ideas I outline here are explored in much greater depth in that book. I will therefore reference relevant passages at appropriate points.

2   I have also examined the theoretical-historical roots of negative critique more extensively elsewhere; see Flügel-Martinsen, *Negative Kritik*.

Critical Interrogations: Politics and the Political

Few distinctions in contemporary political theory have received as much attention as that between politics (*la politique*) and the political (*le politique*).[3] Yet what is often overlooked is that this distinction does not represent a single, coherent theoretical program. Different authors employ it in distinct ways, and in some cases, significant tensions exist between these interpretations.[4] Despite these differences, however, many of these approaches do share a fundamental concern: Whether in Lefort's attempt to redefine political philosophy, Mouffe's agonistic theory of democracy, or Rancière's distinction—differing in terminology but closely related in substance—between policing (*la police*) and politics (*la politique*), all of these perspectives emphasize, with considerable force, both the ways in which existing institutional orders can be questioned and the role that critically interrogative practices play in challenging them, as well as the constitutive function of the political in shaping social order. If we follow these different thinkers, it becomes clear that understanding the potential for change within political institutions is not just a matter of critical analysis—it requires, on a much more fundamental level, understanding this dynamic as *political* in its own right.

---

3   See, for example, Lefort, *Democracy and Political Theory*; Mouffe, *The Return of the Political* and *On the Political*; Breckman, *Adventures of the Symbolic*, 147–158; Flügel, Heil, and Hetzel, *Die Rückkehr des Politischen*; Bedorf and Röttgers, *Das Politische und die Politik*; Bröckling and Feustel, *Das Politische denken*; Marchart, *Post-foundational Political Thought*; Martinsen, *Politik und Politisches*; Flügel-Martinsen, *Radikale Demokratietheorien*, Chapter 3.

4   For my interpretation of the distinction between politics and the political, see Oliver Flügel-Martinsen, *Befragungen des Politischen*, Chapter 3.1. There, I provide a critical analysis of left-Heideggerian readings of this distinction, such as those found in Chantal Mouffe's approach. In my view, such readings promote a political ontologization of conflict, which undermines attempts to theorize the political with an awareness of contingency and from a post-essentialistic perspective.

At first glance, this may seem like an obvious point, but it carries significant implications. To truly understand political structures—and political orders more broadly—we must consider how they originally came into being, the processes and mechanisms through which they were constituted, and, just as importantly, how they might be transformed or even dismantled. Political thought is thus required to examine both institutional dimensions and those that extend constitutively beyond existing institutions: It relies, in short, on a critical interrogation of the present informed by a theory of society. This analytic focus, with its constitutively dual perspective, is conceptually reflected in the distinction between politics and the political (or, in Rancière's parallel distinction, between police order and politics): According to this distinction, politics (in Rancière's terms: *la police*) represents the institutional perspective oriented toward an existing political order. In contrast, the concept of the political (in Rancière's terms: *la politique*) addresses the dimensions of political practice that always exceed this institutional perspective—practices that bring institutions into being in the first place or, in many cases, open up existing institutional orders to a contest over meaning and significance.

The distinction between politics and the political thus allows us to conceive of the very formation of social and political orders as a political process. More importantly, it draws attention to practices that challenge and question existing orders. Rancière expresses this distinction between the two dimensions with particular clarity, though using different terminology: At the level of order—what Rancière calls policing—we are dealing with "the set of procedures whereby the aggregation and consent of activities is achieved, the organization of powers, the distribution of places and roles, and the systems for legitimizing this distribution."[5] The extrainstitutional dimension of the political, however, disrupts this established structure: "Political activity is whatever shifts a body from the place assigned to it or changes a place's destination. It makes visible what had no business being seen, and makes heard a discourse where once there was only place for noise; it makes understood as

---

5   Rancière, *Disagreement*, 28.

discourse what was once only heard as noise."[6] This makes possible, first, a form of political thought that is not confined to institutional processes but is capable of understanding the political constitution of sociopolitical orders in its entirety. And second, this conception of the political strongly underscores that the interrogation of existing orders is itself a constitutive feature of the political. Lefort, in particular, has consistently emphasized that the being of the world is not fixed once and for all, nor does it have a stable structure around which political orders are built. Rather, the being of the world itself is open to critical political interrogation and is therefore revealed as something that can be shaped.[7] We will return to this point below.

The political itself must therefore be understood as a practice of critical interrogation. Distinguishing between politics and the political, or with Rancière between policing and politics, allows us to conceptually capture the tension between institutional structures and a practice that both precedes and exceeds them, highlighting the political as an inherently critical and transformative force. When thinkers such as Lefort and Rancière—in different but related ways—argue for the rediscovery of this kind of practice against the dominant perspectives of political science, political sociology,[8] or even the whole tradition of political thought, they are ultimately trying to expose the dual role of the political as both creative and disruptive.[9] As Rancière's reflections illustrate, this understanding of the political also challenges binaries commonly found in the social sciences, such as the opposition between structural theories and those based on agency. At stake here are both sides of the coin—the political order with its associated normative structures, and subject positions. These are reshaped through a practice of critical interrogation; they are carried out by actors who subvert established ways of experiencing the world through acts of defiance—and who, by politically subjectivizing themselves in new and unexpected ways, fight for a new distribution of the

---

6   Rancière, *Disagreement*, 30.

7   See Lefort, "The Permanence of the Theologico-Political."

8   See Lefort, "The Question of Democracy."

9   See Rancière, *Disagreement*, Chapter 4.

sensible (*partage du sensible*).[10] This concept of Rancière's, of the distribution of the sensible, describes social and political structures as systems that regulate what can be seen and said—structures that profoundly shape, and in fact constitute, our perception of the world. These structures determine "that a particular activity is visible and another is not, that this speech is understood as discourse and another as noise."[11] Emancipatory politics, then, must work to shift and reconfigure the experiential framework of a given distribution of the sensible.

In my view, this practice-centered approach to political resistance and subject displacement also benefits from perspectives that do not explicitly rely on the distinction between politics and the political, nor necessarily develop it in detail. One key reference here is Foucault's work on subject formation within discursive power structures and the development of practices of resistance that push back against hegemonic discourses through counterdiscourses. Also relevant is the performative theory of political resistance that builds on his ideas—a framework to which Judith Butler has increasingly turned their attention in recent years.[12]

What seems crucial to emphasize here, though, is that recognizing the contested nature of world-ordering does not necessarily mean that the political must be defined as ontologically conflictual. In this respect, different theories of the political diverge considerably. As I have discussed in greater detail elsewhere,[13] contemporary debates reveal at least two distinct ways of conceptualizing the political. On one side are approaches influenced by a left-Heideggerian tradition, which interpret the distinction between politics and the political through the lens of Heidegger's ontological

---

10   See Rancière, *The Politics of Aesthetics* and *Disagreement*.

11   Rancière, *Disagreement*, 29.

12   See Foucault, *Subject and Power*; Butler, *Notes Toward a Performative Theory of Assembly*. I explore the importance of Foucault and Butler's perspectives for this context in various sections of my study *Befragungen des Politischen* (see Chapters 2.4, 3.2, and 3.3).

13   See Flügel-Martinsen, *Befragungen des Politischen*, Chapter 3.1. Further references can be found there.

difference between beings and being[14]—thereby assigning an inherently antagonistic structure to the political. In my view, this interpretation—most prominently articulated in the work of Chantal Mouffe—not only contradicts the postessentialist and, as we will soon examine more closely, fundamentally contingent nature of the political, but also results in an ontological overemphasis on conflict. As Rancière's work demonstrates, however, it is entirely possible to conceptualize the political without presupposing an inherent, ontologically privileged antagonism.[15] To fully grasp the radical potential of the political as a space of critical interrogation and transformation—indeed, as intrinsically so—it suffices to highlight the contingency and lack of fixed foundations in social and political orders[16]

Contingency: Uncertainty and Groundlessness

The idea that social and political orders are contingent is not a novel feature of recent political thought. Rather, it draws on a long intellectual tradition. In fact, one might argue that critical theory only becomes possible once the contingency of social and political structures—and, along with it, the contingency of how we conceptualize the world—comes into focus. There is good reason to see Hegel and Marx (with their critiques of social structures) and Nietzsche (with his critiques of science and morality) as pivotal figures in this development.[17] Each, in different ways, constructs a conceptual toolkit for thinking

---

14   On this point, see Marchart, *Post-foundational Political Thought*.

15   For the perspective that the political is inherently antagonistic, see Mouffe, *Political*, Chapter 2.

16   It is worth noting that Mouffe also acknowledges the contingency of the political. See Mouffe, *Political*, 17–18. She nonetheless maintains that the political is fundamentally structured by conflict.

17   See Flügel-Martinsen, *Befragungen des Politischen*, Chapter 2.1–2.1. Twentieth-century theory has expanded on this in many ways—one need only think of the contributions of Foucault, Derrida, or Rorty.

contingency—one that enables a reflective distancing from both institutional structures and ingrained patterns of thought. By revealing how social and conceptual orders came to be, these thinkers strip them of their assumed permanence, making them available for critical interrogation and, ultimately, transformation. While Hegel's philosophy still bears strong traces of reconciliation and positions averse to critique,[18] his work nonetheless insists on historical change as the dominant force.[19] For Hegel, this force is so fundamental that no foundation, however secure, can fully escape it. And from Hegel, it is only a short step to Marx's perspective, which sees historical change as something driven by active struggle—a position already systematically introduced in many passages in Hegel's writings. Both thinkers, however, go beyond social structures and extend their analysis to knowledge itself—recognizing that even epistemic frameworks are contingent.[20] Nietzsche pushes this insight further, exposing the contingency of knowledge so profoundly that even the illusion of objective, neutral science dissolves. Engagement with these ideas—whether in agreement or critique—has not only shaped Frankfurt School critical theory but continues to serve as a steady undercurrent in the broader discourses that sustain contemporary political thought.[21] What makes these approaches critical theories is their ability to demonstrate that both social and epistemic orders are fundamentally malleable—keeping open the possibility of continual critical interrogation and critique. For as soon as we recognize that the structures of knowledge, perception, and social life are contingent, they lose their claim to inevitability—and the possibility of things being otherwise flashes into view.

---

18   See Adorno, "Critique," 282–283.

19   See, for example, Hegel's reflections on how history fundamentally structures institutions: Hegel, *Elements of the Philosophy of Right*, section 3.

20   See also Hegel's pointed remark that even the categories of logic must be understood as subject to historical change: Hegel, *The Science of Logic*, 30–31.

21   Adorno, in particular, repeatedly stressed the importance of Nietzsche for his own critical thought. See Adorno, *Problems of Moral Philosophy*, Lecture 17.

In my view, what makes the discourse of the political such an invaluable resource for critical theory is its ability to think contingency in the most radical sense *while also* recognizing the full scope of possibilities that arise from it—without relying on deeper assumptions about historical progress, a dynamic of conflict or revolution declared inevitable by a philosophy of history, or a specific politicosocial ontology. Lefort offers an important insight here: There is an avowedly intimate connection between becoming aware of epistemic uncertainty and recognizing the contingency of political and social realities.[22] To be clear: Contingency does not suddenly emerge where there was once immutability. Rather, conditions that were previously seen as fixed can come to be perceived as changeable—and, by extension, as fundamentally contingent. Lefort locates this shift in what he calls the democratic age, a period defined by the French Revolution and, in particular, the symbolic execution of the monarchy. With this democratic age, Lefort argues, comes a process he describes as the dissolution of the reference points of certainty (*dissolution des repères de la certitude*).[23] This idea aligns with Lefort's well-known thesis that the space of political power in democracy is empty[24]—empty in the sense emphasized by contingency theory, meaning power is no longer permanently occupied or grounded in a fixed order of meaning, since its stability is always subject to change and uncertainty. Under these conditions, critical political practice becomes possible, as power, law, and knowledge are continually "called into question."[25] Rancière's rethinking of global structures and subject positions should be understood in precisely this way: as following from an interrogation of existing conditions, which in turn highlights the contingency of social and political orders. From his perspective, politics—understood as the practice of shaping the world through

---

22   Lefort, "La dissolution des repères et l'enjeu démocratique."

23   Lefort, "Démocratie et avènement d'un 'lieu vide,'" 463.

24   See Lefort, "Démocratie et avènement d'un 'lieu vide,'" 465.

25   Lefort, "Reversibility: Political Freedom and the Freedom of the Individual," 179.

conflict—is a direct outcome of this contingency. Politics exists because it has no fixed foundation.[26]

Negative Critique

The similarities between recent discourse on the political and Adorno's ideas about critical theory, to which I gestured at in the opening sections of this chapter, are perhaps nowhere more apparent than in a brief essay by Adorno titled "Critique."[27] In this piece, Adorno not only forcefully defends the importance, legitimacy, and even necessity of negative forms of critique, but also immediately connects them to a concept of politics and democracy that closely aligns with the ideas I have been exploring here. One could even argue that Adorno is, in effect, laying out the foundations of a critical theory of the political in its preliminary form. At the outset, he implicitly anticipates—at least in part—the distinction between politics and the political, or between police order and politics, by stating that "politics is not a self-enclosed, isolated sphere, as it manifests itself for instance in political institutions, procedures, and procedural rules, but rather can be conceived only in its relationship to the societal play of forces."[28] For this reason, Adorno contends, critique cannot be limited to "a narrow political field"[29]—meaning the sphere of political operations in the strictest sense—but must instead extend to the broader social realm. Similar operations and an equally broad focus are also central to the political practices centered on critical interrogation that we encountered above in thinkers such as Lefort and Rancière. Much like Lefort and Rancière, Adorno also inscribes this political critique into the very concept of democracy, which he ultimately

---

26   See Rancière, *Disagreement*, 16.

27   Adorno, *Critique*. The essay was originally published on 27 June 1969—just weeks before Adorno's death—as a piece aimed at a broader audience in the weekly newspaper *Die Zeit*.

28   Adorno, *Critique*, 281.

29   Adorno, *Critique*, 281.

conceives of as a form of critical political practice. For him, the relationship between democracy and critique "is demonstrated in the power to resist established opinions and, at the same time, to resist existing institutions—to resist everything that is merely posited, that justifies itself by its mere existence."[30] As with Lefort and Rancière, Adorno is ultimately asserting the contingency of existing institutions and systems of belief, along with a demand that they be critically interrogated—and thus, ultimately, that we recognize their potential to be transformed. What Adorno makes unmistakably clear is, moreover, why critique must allow itself to be limited, if necessary, to a purely negative approach. Adorno argues that the demand to make critique dependent on its constructive potential ultimately serves to blunt its critical edge:

> One continually finds the word *critique*, if it is tolerated at all, ac-companied by the word *constructive*. The insinuation is that only someone can practice critique who can propose something better than what is being criticized ... By making the positive a condition for it, critique is tamed from the very beginning and loses its ve-hemence.[31]

A similar trend can be observed in contemporary political phi-losophy, particularly in the way debates in political theory and international political theory on justice often expect critical posi-tions to provide normative justifications.[32] Raymond Geuss—the most prominent contemporary advocate of this position—rightly insists, in my view, that critique must firmly reject any demand that it be constructive.[33] For the purposes of this discussion, what

---

30   Adorno, *Critique*, 281–282.

31   Adorno, *Critique*, 287.

32   See Chapter 6. For my critique of this approach to political theory, see also Flügel-Martinsen, *Die Normativitätsbegründungsfalle: Die unterschätzte Bedeutung befragender und negativer Kritikformen in der Politischen Theorie und der Internationalen Politischen Theorie*.

33   See Geuss, *Philosophy and Real Politics* and Geuss, "Must Criticism be Constructive?"

is particularly striking about Geuss's argument is his claim that the demand for constructiveness serves as a tool to neutralize critique of existing social structures—or even worse: that it allows "the existing social formation to dictate the terms in which it can be criticised."[34] In short, the question of negative critique concerns whether critical political practice—essential to developing a critical theory of the political—is possible at all. Rancière's concept of *la part des sans-part*—those who have no share in the existing order of the sensible, whose voices are dismissed as noise, and who are relegated to invisibility[35]—describes precisely those who struggle politically for a redistribution of the world's structures. They should not—and, in fact, cannot—be expected to have a blueprint ready for an alternative or more just world. After all, the power of interrogative critique lies precisely in its ability to work negatively: The *part of those without a part* fights for a world defined by conditions that cannot yet even be described—let alone justified or legitimized—within the current order. The essence of this negatively interrogative political critique is captured in Foucault's assertion that critique is the art of "not being governed *like that*."[36] This formulation calls for a form of resistance that does not need to have a ready-made vision of how governance or forms of government should function differently. More importantly, it must not—and cannot—be restrained by the demand for a constructive alternative. James Tully articulates the radical-democratic implications inherent to this notion of critique. It points first, he argues, to a conception of philosophy and theory that is fundamentally interwoven with practices constituting civil

---

34   Geuss, *Philosophy and Real Politics*, 96.

35   Both historically and in the present, the mechanisms of exclusion from speech and visibility are clearly evident in the experiences of those without a part: One need only think of the noise traditionally associated with the lower classes, the irrationality ascribed to the speech of women or racially oppressed minorities, or the exclusion from public life that women in patriarchal societies experience as a consequence of being confined to the household—or that *sans-papiers* face today because their lack of legal status forces them into illegality.

36   Foucault, "What Is Critique," 384.

society. The philosopher's critical engagement accordingly does not differ from that of an active citizen; both take part in a collective questioning of existing "forms of government."[37] Second, this process is then an essential part "of the practices of freedom of the governed (as active agents) that are put into action in response [to the forms of government]."[38] In some ways, this echoes Adorno's idea that theory itself is a form of practice—though without his deep reservations about political activism, of which he remained skeptical.[39]

The crucial point here is that this political critique must be seen as a specific form of critique which, building on Foucault, can be described as subversive. Its force comes from a relentless practice of critical interrogation—one that refuses to be bound by the demand for constructiveness. For this mode of critique, the act of challenging is not a sign of deficiency; rather, it is the very source of its intensity and democratic resilience. In terms of intellectual lineage, Nietzsche's genealogy plays a foundational role—Foucault's own critical project, which he also calls genealogy, draws on it, as do Derrida's mode of deconstruction and Adorno's rejection of the imperative to be constructive.[40] In the strands of contemporary political theory and philosophy that I am pulling together here as a critical theory of the political, a certain mode of negative inquiry plays a particularly important role. Even though these approaches differ from one another—and I do not claim that they all stem from the same theoretical roots—this shared focus on negative inquiry remains central. It is this form of critique that keeps alive the potential for a dynamic of political resistance in the face of hegemonic power. And it is among the key tasks of a critical theory of the political to participate in this practice of resistance by relentlessly interrogating the present.

---

37   Tully, *Public Philosophy as Critical Activity*, 22.

38   Tully, *Public Philosophy as Critical Activity*, 22.

39   See Adorno, "Marginalia to Theory and Praxis."

40   All three thinkers—famously—return to Nietzsche. See Adorno, *Problems of Moral Philosophy*; Foucault, "Nietzsche, Genealogy, History"; Derrida, *The Politics of Friendship*.

3. Beyond Truth? Truth Skepticism and the Horizons of Radical Democracy

Perspectives skeptical of truth, which are central to the interrogations of the present at the core of this essay, have consistently drawn heavy criticism and rejection in recent theoretical discourse. And yet, despite objections often raised in the name of rationality, and especially in the name of a rationality rooted in Enlightenment traditions, such approaches have nevertheless emerged over the past several decades as a visible and influential critical paradigm across the humanities, the social sciences, and cultural studies. In newer disciplines such as gender studies, postcolonial studies, and cultural studies, these approaches have even become decisive. Michel Foucault was among the first to argue that such skepticism does not abandon the Enlightenment's critical tradition but rather radicalizes it. Instead of resting on assumptions of rationality, it pulls those very assumptions into a process of critical interrogation—a hallmark of Enlightenment thinking itself. In this way, Foucault both aligned himself with Kant's philosophical legacy and pushed beyond its rationalist form of critique, using genealogical methods to trace how our ideas of rationality are bound up with relations of power.[1] Skepticism about truth thus takes on a broader scope. It not only opposes essentialist conceptions of truth, such as those in onto-logical theories of truth since Plato or the metaphysical–rationalist models of modernity (as found, for instance, in Descartes), but also challenges more recent attempts (most notably by Jürgen Habermas) to redefine truth in terms of rational acceptability as intersubjective

---

1   See Foucault, "What Is Critique" and "What Is Enlightenment?"

agreement, thereby both questioning and preserving the claim to truth.[2]

It is precisely this expansive reach that has, in recent years, prompted renewed suspicious of postessentialist forms of skepticism about truth. Today, these approaches are once again meeting resistance, fueled by a mix of epistemological doubts, competing interests within the scientific community, and political anxieties—and this despite that fact that they had seemed, after the heated debates of the 1980s, to secure a stable place within critical theory. Like everything else, the philosophy of science is subject to trends: Once seen as the vanguard of epistemology, approaches skeptical of truth have now begun to lose ground to calls for a return to more concrete theories of truth—often paired with sharp critiques of doubts about truth, tout court.[3] But when such approaches are questioned even from within philosophy, the pressure only intensifies—under an even stronger attack from a recent shift in science policy driven by a much more reductive understanding of knowledge. In the age of academic capitalism,[4] universities are increasingly reliant on third-party funding, and this economic shift favors a model of research rooted in straightforward, empirical assumptions about truth. Contrary to Paul Boghossian's claims about the dominance of truth skepticism, the prevailing standard across the humanities and social sciences now leans toward a much simpler understanding of theory—especially in quantitatively driven research. These research projects are often generally guided by a plain idea of truth: One formulates hypotheses, tests them empirically, and uses an implicit correspondence theory of truth to determine what is the case, and what is not. There is no space for skepticism in this model—not because it has been disproved, but because it is being economically outcompeted by the promise of funding for data-driven, empirically grounded research. Still, more than market logic and intellectual fashion is at work here. A third, political dimension

---

2   See Habermas, *Truth and Justification.*

3   See the paradigmatic presentation of this argument in Boghossian, *Fear of Knowledge.*

4   See Münch, *Academic Capitalism.*

seems crucial: According to a common critique, skepticism about truth is itself said to have paved the way for post-truth politics and authoritarian populism. This dynamic has only intensified in recent years, especially given the rising authority of natural science models in addressing global crises (such as climate change or the coronavirus pandemic) where empirical evidence plays a vital role in shaping public policy.

Because this exerts pressure on theoretical approaches that are skeptical of truth—not only by denying them legitimacy, but also by suspecting them of enabling right-wing populist and authoritarian movements—it seems to me that a more detailed reflection is warranted. Specifically, we need to consider the subjects of truth and skepticism about truth, and how they relate to a critical theory of the present. Only then can the following chapters examine the practical, critical potential of these tools in political theory through more concrete interrogations. The first step is to sketch, in broad strokes, the structure of the epistemological suspicion and the accompanying political-normative critique. The next is to demonstrate that truth-skeptical inquiries not only pose no threat to forms of democratic politics rooted in freedom, but that the democratic era itself bears marks of skepticism about truth—making skeptical, interrogative approaches almost ideally suited to revealing the radically democratic nature of emancipatory politics, whose very possibility is founded on a departure from the pursuit of absolute truth and certainty.

In an essay devoted to analyzing the present, however, it is crucial to consider yet another dimension: the challenges brought about by crises that stem from natural threats, even if their root causes are so-cietal, as is especially evident in the climate crisis or the coronavirus pandemic. In the face of such crises and challenges, must not the role of empirically verified, objective truths be reevaluated entirely? And is this not especially so, inasmuch as conspiracy-fueled doubts about climate change or the pandemic have been aggressively stoked by the political right? In such a situation, one must urgently ask whether skepticism toward truth is simply irresponsible.

Even before the climate crisis and the coronavirus pandemic, the public largely took a view of science as the natural sciences.

But today, in serious mainstream democratic discourse, that model has become almost uncontested. That does not mean that natural science methods are accepted without criticism, as the widespread public presence of antiscience rhetoric, which often crosses into full-blown conspiracy theory, makes clear. Recent attacks by the Trump administration against universities and science even prove that such antiscience positions can become the official policy of an important country such as the United States.

Still, when people speak of science or scientific knowledge today, there is little doubt that they mean science in the mold of the hard sciences—while alternative models of knowledge production, including ones skeptical of truth, are rarely even acknowledged. This was especially clear in public discourse about the pandemic, particularly when experts called for input from disciplines beyond those directly involved with epidemiology and virology. When it came to policy decisions such as reopening schools or childcare centers, for instance, experts from educational science, psychology, or sociology were also consulted. But even then, the expectations placed on these disciplines were framed by a positivist model of science—what was sought were generalizable, fact-based observations. These disciplines—in this case, the social sciences—were defined within that framework not by their unique ways of thinking or reflecting, but merely by their different subject matter.

Is that approach—especially in a moment like ours, in which urgent issues such as climate change seem to demand firm empirical knowledge—perhaps the only viable one? Could crises such as the climate emergency or the recent pandemic actually serve as a clarifying shock, forcing us to focus on what really matters? And do perspectives such as mine—rooted in a critical political theory that is skeptical of objectivity and truth—now appear to be a kind of intellectual luxury, out of place in the face of today's urgent problems? Do crises with origins in natural processes—such as rising temperatures or the transmission of a virus to humans—change everything, even when they are socially caused or coproduced? These are questions I will return to at the end of this chapter.

Truth Skepticism Under Suspicion

Back in the mid-2000s—about a decade before approaches skeptical of truth associated with so-called French Theory began to be publicly blamed, starting in the mid-2010s, for enabling right-wing populist post-truth narratives in Western democracies—Paul Boghossian published a short, polemical text aimed at thoroughly discrediting what he called social constructivism.[5] Under this rubric, Boghossian loosely groups together a wide array of constructivist, deconstructive, genealogical, and discourse-theoretical approaches. Rather than engage them through detailed analysis, he references them selectively, using isolated examples to confront what he considers to be decisive, systematic objections. He justifies lumping these disparate positions together on the grounds that they all share what he identifies as a basic consensus—one that he sees as the dominant paradigm of human knowledge in the humanities and social sciences (vi). According to Boghossian, that consensus rests on the claim "that knowledge is socially constructed" (vi). There are, of course, good reasons to challenge the idea—assumed by Boghossian—that this outlook holds a dominant position in the humanities and social sciences. As I observed above, many influential empirical studies, whether explicitly or implicitly, still rely on a more realist, correspondence-based theory of truth—the idea that truth is simply what is the case. Still, whether these truth-skeptical approaches are in fact central or marginal is not actually relevant to Boghossian's argument. He is not concerned with describing the field empirically but with systematically rejecting these perspectives. More crucial, then, are the specific features Boghossian attributes to what he sees as the core of the social-constructivist consensus. At its heart, he claims, is a doctrine of equal validity—one that insists "that there are many other, radically different yet equally valid ways of knowing the world, with science being just one of them" (4).

---

5   Boghossian, *Fear of Knowledge*. Page numbers that follow appear in parentheses in the text and, unless stated otherwise, refer to this book.

Boghossian argues that this doctrine is based on the idea that there can be no higher authority for judging the truth of different perspectives, since knowledge is always contextual (5–6) and cannot be verified or disproved by appealing to external facts. This standpoint implies a form of fact-constructivism—the belief that there are no facts that exist independently of our interpretations. Boghossian sees this as a mistake. While he concedes that some social phenomena—his example is homosexuality—may be shaped by cultural narratives, he firmly rejects the idea that this applies to "facts about mountains, dinosaurs or electrons" (26).

We do not need to dig into the finer points of Boghossian's argument here. What matters more for our purposes are his initial assumptions and the political and normative implications he draws from this stylized version of social constructivism. Taken together, these lead to a climate of suspicion toward any truth-skeptical theory. Worse, such theories are now seen as incapable of offering meaningful criticism of political stances or social realities. Boghossian suggests that this kind of social-constructivist thinking has serious and unavoidable consequences. While it might have epistemologically liberating potential when it highlights the contingency of social norms we wrongly take as natural—provided it stays grounded in "the standard canons of good scientific reasoning" (130)—it loses its critical edge when it moves beyond that scope. Once it steps beyond the narrowly circumscribed framework of scientific rationality and methodology—once it expands its assumptions about contingency and adopts a broader perspectivism—it forfeits its critical thrust, or can only preserve it at the cost of blatant inconsistencies in the form of a double standard:

> [F]or if the powerful can't criticize the oppressed, because the central epistemological categories are inexorably tied to particular perspectives, it also follows that the oppressed cannot criticize the powerful. The only remedy, so far as I can see, for what threatens to be a strongly conservative upshot, is to accept an overt double standard: allow a questionable idea to be criticized if it is held by those in a position of power—Christian creationism,

for example—but not if it is held by those whom the powerful
oppress—Zuni creationism, for example. (130)

This sketch of what Boghossian sees as the fatal—yet unavoidable—consequences of truth-skeptical positions lines up structurally
with the objection raised by Zurich philosopher Michael Hampe in
a guest piece for the German weekly *DIE ZEIT*. There, Hampe
addresses the current crisis in public discourse and decision-
making culture in Western democracies, brought about by right-
wing populists' strategic use of post-truth rhetoric. Like Boghossian,
Hampe builds an umbrella category, speaking broadly of the
cultural-studies Left, which—just like Boghossian's version of
social constructivism—is marked by truth-relativist positions.
Hampe argues that this camp must now be waking up with a kind
of hangover, having not only failed to mount a defense against the
lying, brutish Right, but in effect having cleared the way for its rise.[6]

What response can a political theory skeptical of truth offer
here? Against these sweeping accusations, it can be shown—and
this will be one of the primary aims of the following chapters—that
tools such as Foucault's genealogy or Derrida's deconstruction,
and similar methods, are uniquely capable of launching a critically
subversive interrogation of the present allowing us to dissolve
categories that appear natural and unquestionable. Boghossian
himself acknowledges this emancipatory potential—citing, for
example, the work of Simone de Beauvoir and Anthony Appiah (130).
But unlike his insistence that this potential only emerges when
"the standard canons of good scientific reasoning" (130) remain
untouched, genealogical and deconstructive strategies draw their
critical power precisely from their refusal to stop at inherited
methodologies and epistemic forms—instead exposing their
entanglement with social power dynamics and asymmetries. Unlike
what Boghossian and Hampe suggest, doubting truth as a reference
point does not strip inquiry of its critical potential—it actually
makes critique possible in the first place. In *Tympan*,[7] for example,

---

6   See Hampe, "Katerstimmung bei den pubertären Theoretikern."
7   See Derrida, "Tympan."

Derrida shows how the seemingly neutral philosophical work of conceptual distinctions and classifications actually operates within a mode of domination—one that imposes hierarchies through acts of categorization and renders these power structures invisible by dressing them up as purely conceptual moves. This gives philosophy the appearance of objectivity and truth-seeking, the kind Plato already claimed was situated beyond the messy realm of human striving and everyday life.[8] What matters here is that these critically interrogative practices—contrary to Boghossian's assumption and the impression Hampe gives—do not rely on external anchors such as the category of truth in order to be effective. Nor are they rendered incapable of critique, or reduced to mere arbitrariness or partisanship, simply because they reject such reference points. In *Rogues*, Derrida makes an important remark—tucked away in a footnote—that deconstruction does not come from the outside. Rather, it traces what we might call the autodeconstruction that confronts categories and concepts from within—especially those that try to present themselves as solid, stable, or beyond question.[9] This applies not only to ontological and metaphysical concepts of truth, but also to seemingly more flexible categories such as criteria for rational acceptability[10]—and crucially, also to politically loaded referents such as the nation or an ethnically (or racially) defined people, which play a major role in today's right-wing populist discourse and underwrite their aggressive and often violent exclusionary politics.

If, following Foucault, we understand social regimes of meaning and truth as discourses whose epistemic certainty is grounded in hegemonic power formations, then these regimes can be subjected to genealogical critique. This approach replaces their putative stability or timeless validity with an account of their historically contingent formation, as the result of social and political struggles

---

8   Plato famously justifies his ideal of rule by a philosopher king in this way; see Plato, *Republic*, 500a–b.

9   See Derrida, *Rogues*, 173–174n14.

10   See also Derrida, *Monolingualism of the Other*, on the deconstruction of rational argumentation.

over interpretive dominance.[11] Similar gestures of degrounding can be carried out through Derrida's deconstructive strategies—a point we will return to when discussing the deconstruction of national identity. There it will become evident that deconstruction plays a crucial role in undermining substantialist presuppositions about collective identity—such as the notion of a fixed or unified "Volk" or "people"—that are central to right-wing populist politics (see Chapter 5).

More broadly, I would argue that a crucial distinction between critical positions skeptical of truth and populist post-truth claims is being deliberately obscured in both academic and public discourse: While the latter tend to jump to the unreflective conclusion that their own claims cannot be challenged—as there is supposedly no such thing as scientifically grounded truth—genealogical and deconstructive strategies lead instead to a thoroughgoing commitment to critical interrogation, which always includes a reflexive questioning of one's own assumptions and methodological procedures. It is precisely this reflexive self-critique that populist and authoritarian movements routinely reject. Yet this marks a decisive difference—one reason why the claim that truth-skepticism gives rise to post-truth discourse is not only wildly exaggerated but also serves to discredit a potent form of critique. This is a form of critique that can be wielded just as effectively against populist post-truth rhetoric as against right-wing essentialist constructions of "the people" or "the nation." Contrary to Boghossian's assertion, it is simply not the case that positions which reject truth as a point of reference are thereby forced to treat all perspectives as equally valid. Quite the opposite: By means of a needling strategy of continuous interrogation, they can destabilize positions that attempt to shield themselves from scrutiny—while at the same time submitting both others and themselves to critical questioning and reflexive self-interrogation. Hence there is no reason for the cultural-studies Left to be experiencing a hangover; what is needed is to sharpen its tools

---

11   A condensed version of this discursive-theoretical and genealogical critique of the given can already be found in Foucault's inaugural lecture at the Collège de France: Foucault, *The Order of Discourse*.

of critique and put their force to work on concrete phenomena. This is the purpose of the critical interrogation of the present offered in this essay. Before we turn to the examples of neoliberal hegemony and the rise of populism (Chapter 4), the return of exclusionary politics (Chapter 5), and the interrogation of a globally unjust border regime (Chapter 6), it is helpful to briefly sketch out the truth-skeptical contours of the democratic age and hint at the radically democratic potential inherent in acts of critical interrogation. This will also allow us to begin illuminating certain key questions and thematic areas that will be taken up in more detail in the chapters that follow.

Contingency and the Loss of Truth: The Democratic Age and the Horizons of Radical Democracy

Claude Lefort repeatedly emphasized that the political must be understood as a process by which society constitutes itself politically. In much the same way, Rancière's reflections on the political constitution of the world can be read as a call to recognize the political production of social arrangements. Both thinkers especially underscore the enduring possibility of critically inter-rogating existing institutional orders[12]—a process through which transformation, and at times even subversion, becomes possible. Such openings and reconfigurations are possible precisely because, as Rancière puts it, "the foundation of politics" lies in "the lack of a foundation."[13] Human societies are not anchored in any higher or transcendent truth; they are contingent. And this contingency does not just apply to the content of political orders; it also extends

---

12   As should already be clear (see above, Chapter 2), this is not a view limited to the political thought of Lefort and Rancière. The practice of critical interrogation plays a central role across a broader field of positions that either fall within the discourse of the political and radical democracy or are directly shaped by it. On the role of such critique within the discourse of radical democracy, see Flügel-Martinsen, *Kritik*.

13   Rancière, *Disagreement*, 16.

to their procedural forms and to the norms that structure those procedures. All of it is therefore always open to contestation. What makes the democratic age distinctive is that it renders visible the fact that social order is situated beyond truth.

Lefort's analyses of the relationship between democracy and totalitarianism strike me as a particularly instructive way of approaching this problem. Lefort initially describes the democratic age as an epoch in which the contingency of political and social institutions becomes perceptible. The diagnosis of contingency discussed above (see Chapter 2) does not mean that societies only became contingent at a certain point in time, while they previously were not. Rather, it points to a form of self-relation: Democratic societies describe themselves as contingent. This becoming-conscious of contingency is thus the historical novelty. And it is for this reason that the center of power in these societies is empty in any meaning-generating sense: What these societies institutionalize is not embodied power but the conflict over the occupation of the position of power as a permanent conflict.[14] This makes democratic society a "society without a body"[15]—and subjects it to the enduring interrogation discussed above.

Yet it is precisely this absence of embodiment—and the resulting disjunction, which Lefort sees as crucial to democratic theory, between temporary power-holders and civil society[16]— that subjects both power-holders and the institutions they occupy to ongoing critical scrutiny, while also creating the potential for attempts to symbolically reembody power through ideology. Lefort describes this as a totalitarian temptation[17]—one that democracy is not only exposed to, but which arises precisely from the uncertainty that defines the democratic age. Only where the absence of embodied fullness is felt can the desire arise to overcome it. The totalitarianism on which Lefort focuses—like other attempts at ideological filling, which today manifest in religious

---

14   See Lefort, "The Question of Democracy," 17–18.

15   Lefort, "The Question of Democracy," 18.

16   See Lefort, "Vorwort zu Eléments d'une critique de la bureaucratie," 49–50.

17   See Lefort, "La dissolution des repères et l'enjeu démocratique," 561.

fundamentalisms or the resurgence of nationalist ideologies—is a modern phenomenon, one that emerges from the very epistemic and normative conditions of the democratic age itself. From this perspective, political practice—even in the democratic age—can always slip into nondemocratic temptations. There is no cure-all for this, not even reliably stable institutional safeguards, since democratic practice, as Lefort's reflections also suggest, depends precisely on the flexibility that grows out of conflicts within political institutions and procedures—especially the tension between institutionalized politics and the political sphere that operates beyond fixed structures. Because democratic processes themselves are subject to this same uncertainty, democracy remains, inevitably, a kind of adventure, something we can learn to navigate, but that can always fail again, as both historical shifts from democracy to authoritarian or totalitarian regimes and today's challenges from authoritarian right-wing populist movements powerfully and disturbingly show.

Taking recourse to Lefort, we can draw a clear line between democratic and nondemocratic political practices and demands: Political movements are only democratic if they do not try to eliminate the experience of contingency, the reality of uncertainty, and the constitutive pluralism that comes with it. This gives us a fairly reliable sign that right-wing populist movements merely hijack the language of democracy while actually opposing it: They claim to speak for—or even to embody—the "true people," dismissing all other viewpoints as illegitimate.[18] While we will explore this more thoroughly in the coming chapters, we can already sketch out the basic structure of the radical democratic response to the ways in which authoritarian populist movements and parties co-opt democratic language. One key insight of radical democratic theory is that "the people," as a singular entity, can never be fully represented or defined.[19] Judith Butler makes a vital point when they reject the notion of representing the "entirety of the people" and stresses: "each positing of the people through assembly risks or invites a set

---

18   On this point, see the seminal discussion in Müller, *What Is Populism?*, 40.

19   See Flügel-Martinsen, *Radikale Demokratietheorien*, Chapter 5.2.

of conflicts that, in turn, prompt a growing set of doubts about who the people really are."[20] Hence the real democratic power of public protests in the name of the people lies not in affirming a fixed identity, but in raising questions, sowing doubt, and foregrounding uncertainty. That is why authoritarian populist appeals to "the people" and their attacks on elites do not count as democratic political interventions: They do not interrogate forms of politics that recognize openness and uncertainty, but rather invoke a supposedly higher truth, meant to shut down debate altogether by rendering it superfluous. This in turn justifies the suppression of alternative views, which is exactly what we see when authoritarian populists gain power.

In a similar way, as Jacques Rancière argues, we can distinguish democratic from nondemocratic forms of political subjectivation: Democratic subjectivations challenge the dominant notion of "the people" as fixed within current institutions and semantic orders—what Rancière calls the "police order"—by asserting that the people do not match that image and making demands based on radical equality. Right-wing, antidemocratic movements, by contrast, try to lock down the meaning of "the people" in exclusionary terms. Unlike the essentialist and ethnonationalist notions of the so-called "democratic people" advanced by right-wing populists, approaches to political subjectivation rooted in emancipatory democratic strategies avoid making any substantial claims. Even the idea of equality is not assumed as a given here: The demand for equality stems from an awareness of how contingent the existing "police orders" are—as are the meanings and concepts they uphold. When, as Rancière puts it, "anyone"[21] can challenge the police order or the social order, it is not because they hold some deeper truth—such as claiming to speak for the "real people"—but because their critical interrogation exposes how contingent and thus malleable these orders actually are. That is precisely why the radical democratic implications of political thought that is skeptical of truth and theoretically cognizant of contingency serve as a powerful

---

20   Butler, "We the People," 155.

21   Rancière, *Disagreement*, 15.

argumentative tool against populist post-truth narratives—and not, as is often alleged today, as their handmaiden. The opening toward an uncertain future that comes with such questioning is, as Jacques Derrida has underscored in his reflections on a *démocratie à venir*, one of the core features of democratic practice, a practice that stays true to the always-contested name of democracy and to a future that remains to be shaped. This is a future, crucially, that remains open to the arrival of the Other.[22]

But are these critical acts of interrogation enough to count as democratic practice, or must something else be present to qualify them as such? On the one hand, we have already noted that only those political-democratic challenges count that are willing to acknowledge uncertainty and the inevitable plurality of differing positions. On the other, it has also become clear that this kind of open-ended interrogation is itself a key element of radical democratic practice. So from the standpoint of democratic theory, the question is not what needs to be added to make these interrogations democratic. What is more important is to insist that nothing should be ruled out *a limine*, at the outset, if we want to preserve the possibility of democratic intervention at all. This leads to two key points: a radicalism in both the theory and the practice of democracy; and a self-imposed restraint within democratic theory itself, which serves to protect democracy. To follow James Tully—and as already became clear in our earlier discussion of interrogative, negative critique (see Chapter 2)—a democratic, critical theory of politics must bring its own self-understanding into closer alignment with the practices of civil society. One of Tully's key insights is that theory and practice are two interdependent forms of critical engagement,[23] and that their democratic value lies in their willingness to challenge one another. Only through this mutual openness do theory and practice complement each other. By contrast, any conception of political philosophy or democratic theory that assigns them the role of justifying specific political orders—or even just procedures or norms—must be seen as fundamentally

---

22   See Derrida, *The Politics of Friendship*.

23   See Tully, "Public Philosophy as a Critical Activity."

misplaced, even antipolitical and antidemocratic. As Rancière would argue, such theories are not really about politics at all; they are attempts to bring politics to a close instead of engaging with its democratic possibilities.[24] In this sense, the radical interrogation that drives both theory and practice, and the self-limitation that theory imposes on itself, work together productively: The more theoretical perspective steps down from a position of intellectual supremacy, from which entire blueprints for political order might appear as ultimate goals, the more it can become part of a critical democratic practice that constantly interrogates our institutions, procedures, norms, and shared meanings. These are not fixed once and for all; we continually create them anew; and they must always remain open to revision. This is why conflict and disagreement over norms and procedures are not a problem for democracy; they are essential to its practice.[25] In my view, then, the real question is not whether critical interrogations fall short of what democratic self-rule requires, but whether we have yet carried out enough of these radical interrogations in the name of a radical-democratic future.

Natural Crises and the End of Democratic Truth Skepticism?

Do natural crises (such climate change), or threats tied to environmental exploitation (such as pandemics) spell the end of skepticism about truth? Given the clear need for hard, evidence-based medical and scientific research in the face of challenges such as the climate crisis, or the recent coronavirus pandemic, one might easily think this to be the case. Earlier in this chapter (see above, "Truth Skepticism Under Suspicion"), we examined views that

---

24   See Rancière, *Disagreement*, 62–63. This line of thought also involves a sweeping critique of the long-standing and still-dominant conception of the role of political theory and philosophy as inherited from the history of ideas. For this critique, in addition to the views of Rancière and Tully already discussed, see also Geuss, *Philosophy and Real Politics*.

25   See, pars pro toto, Tully, "The Unfreedom of the Moderns," 110–111.

dismiss any emphasis on contingency—and the skepticism toward truth that it entails—as mere intellectual games, even irresponsible ones. In light of natural crises, one might ask: How can anyone still seriously doubt that objectively verifiable, scientific facts exist, when the evidence is so overwhelming and the dangers so real?

First, it is crucial to clarify that truth-skeptical positions—such as those developed in the wake of Foucault's work[26]—should not be mistaken for the claim that everything is simply arbitrary or meaningless. Foucault's philosophy of science is not about proving that systems of meaning are completely arbitrary; rather, he aims to show that these orders of meaning are also historically shifting—and contested—structures of power. Foucault shows that social and political conditions are equally as contingent as scientific assumptions—that is to say, that they are shaped by historical context—and that both realms are tightly interwoven through power dynamics. He famously explored these tensions using the concept of discourse,[27] which, by definition, involves conflict between competing regimes of truth. Foucault's skepticism about truth does not claim that truth is arbitrary. Instead, it situates truth within historical power relations—relations that uphold certain regimes of veridiction but that can also be challenged. Truth itself, then, must be seen as subject to change.[28]

Put sharply, one could say—following this line of thought—that the debate over truth cannot take place within a supposedly neutral space of scientific discussion, because even the notion of scientific objectivity is itself fundamentally contested. Moreover, this debate does not unfold in a vacuum, free from social influence; it is always already embedded in power dynamics. Skepticism toward truth and objectivity also applies to this very description: It cannot claim to

---

26   See Veyne, *Foucault*, Chapter III.

27   See Foucault, *The Order of Discourse*.

28   For Foucault's discussion of the concept of veridiction, see his analysis of the market as a veridiction regime in his lecture at the Collège de France on January 17, 1979—an analysis he soon expanded to other discursive frameworks: Foucault, *The Birth of Biopolitics: Lectures at the Collège de France 1978–1979*, 14–19.

offer a "truer" account of how orders of knowledge emerge and evolve by appealing to a higher level of understanding; it is itself just one position in an ongoing debate. As Jacques Derrida pointedly argues in *The University Without Condition*, controversies such as these are an essential part of the broader reflective practices in the humanities.[29]

No doubt, especially in the era of climate crisis or in the face of threats such as pandemics, there is a heightened need for scientific research into such phenomena. But to take that as justification for blindly accepting a scientific model of knowledge based on objectivity and so-called factual truth—and to use that as a means of shutting down democratic challenges to claims of truth and objectivity—would be a serious mistake. Indeed, the often contradictory conclusions that arise from scientific studies show us again and again that we are dealing with fundamental issues that cannot simply be solved by doing more research. What is also needed, and what cannot even be approached within a discourse driven by the ideal of objective science, is a critical examination of how our standards—of objectivity, necessity, and the like—are tied to hegemonic systems of meaning and power. Think, for example, of questions such as the following, which cannot be answered by "objective science" alone: Who or what is deemed essential to the system, and why? Who gets more resources as a result? Which responsibilities are seen as private, which as public—and who takes them on, and under which enduring power relations? Whose lives are restricted, to what extent, and for what reasons? And not least: Whose life is put at greater risk, and why?[30] Questions like these call for a serious critique of the standards we use to make judgments, and those standards cannot exclusively be based on empirically verified scientific knowledge.

One key starting point for thinking about such questions can be found in Nietzsche's critical philosophy of science. Nietzsche's critique reaches its peak in the skeptical claim that science—despite

---

29   See Derrida, *The University Without Condition*.

30   See Butler, *Frames of War*, on the vulnerability of life and the unequal distribution of risk.

claiming to replace belief and conviction with insight and objectivity—is ultimately, *contre cœur*, still haunted by the very beliefs and values it claims to have left behind.[31] Science, in this view, is not internally grounded in science itself, but is driven by a kind of belief logic—the very thing it sets out to overcome. This kind of critique of science has taken many forms since then—most notably in the work of Foucault[32] and Habermas[33]—and has repeatedly been used to challenge the natural-scientific model of knowledge. But for the most part, it has had little impact on how the natural sciences see themselves. As long as science continues to ignore the remnants of belief embedded in its supposed objectivity, it shuts itself off from the epistemological tools needed for critical self-reflection. Of course, a politics that blatantly pushes aside scientific knowledge for strategic or manipulative purposes—as authoritarian populism à la Trump aggressively and deliberately does—is clearly one of the most dangerous political developments in the world today. But the right response is not a politics that turns science into a provider of evidence-based expertise and then relies on that to make supposedly neutral, objective decisions.

We owe to Hannah Arendt, among others, the reminder that prejudices—understood as judgments based on preexisting standards—are not automatically problematic in every respect. In fact, they are often necessary for people to carry out and structure both personal and collective relationships to the world in everyday

---

31   See Nietzsche, *The Gay Science*, section 577; see also Flügel-Martinsen, *Jenseits von Glauben und Wissen*, 71–99.

32   Foucault, *The Order of Discourse* and *The Archaeology of Knowledge*.

33   See also Habermas, *Technology and Science as Ideology*. When Habermas and Foucault are mentioned almost in the same breath here, it is important to recognize that there are major differences between them: Foucault offers a discourse analysis and genealogy of scientific rationality that is deeply skeptical of truth—and no longer presents itself, at least not without rupture, as a form of rational science. In contrast, Habermas's critique of the scientific model of knowledge is primarily aimed at defending an alternative understanding of rationality.

life.[34] However, Arendt also stresses an important limit: Judgments made in the mode of prejudice must be kept in check if we are to prevent them from hardening into ideology. Crises—always also times of confusion and a need for orientation—are particularly dangerous in this regard, as they tend to accelerate the solidification and self-reinforcement of prejudices.[35] Parts of Arendt's discussion of "pseudotheories, which, as closed worldviews or ideologies with an explanation for everything, pretend to understand all historical and political reality,"[36] read strikingly like an analysis of today's conspiracy theories, which have grown alarmingly popular in recent years. She shows how these theories take on the shape of a kind of obsessive overapplication of the scientific process of subsuming particulars under general categories: Where judgment, for pragmatic reasons, might apply a standard without questioning the standard itself, conspiracy thinking turns an untested—and untestable—belief into a secret master key to the world. Everything is suddenly made clear to the initiated, while the rest of the world remains in the dark.

Arendt proposes what she sees as the key mode of judgment in situations where our usual standards no longer apply—which, in her view, is the norm in modern life:[37] a kind of judgment without fixed standards, based on the "faculty of judgment"[38] itself. Her reflections on how communities give shape to the world imply that the political space needs a public sphere. But she insists that this public sphere should not be weighed down with issues such as the distribution of economic and social resources; these, she argues in *On Revolution*, are bound up with ideas of needs and wants that can ruin the kind of free, world-making politics she defends.[39] This is, I believe, the point where Arendt's thinking becomes less useful, even problematic for a theory aimed at critically reflecting on standards.

---

34   See Arendt, *The Promise of Politics*, 99–100.

35   See Arendt, *The Promise of Politics*, 102–103.

36   Arendt, *The Promise of Politics*, 103.

37   See Arendt, *The Promise of Politics*, 103–104.

38   Arendt, *The Promise of Politics*, 103.

39   See Arendt, *On Revolution*, Chapter 2.

Her book on revolution, after all, leaves out crucial issues such as social inequality or the racist exploitation and oppression of Black American slaves. That said, one idea from Arendt remains valuable in my view: the notion that standards cannot be critically assessed using other standards—such as, in this case, the standards of scientific objectivity—because those too must be subject to scrutiny. Yet as Foucault's work already makes clear, we cannot imagine a space for public reflection that is somehow detached from social conditions of oppression, exploitation, or inequality. Instead, we must critically examine how standards of judgment—meaning the normative claims, values, or assumptions embedded in how we make meaning—are tied to constellations of power.

The idea that everyday beliefs and truths reflect hegemonic power structures is one of the lasting contributions made by the Italian Marxist Antonio Gramsci to the tradition of critical thinking. For Gramsci, this insight—one that also shapes a critical theory of science and rationality—grew out of a very practical context: the search for effective revolutionary strategies. Pushing back against the common Marxist tendency to reduce politics, culture, and science to mere epiphenomena—or simple reflections—of material conditions, Gramsci highlighted the importance of widely shared beliefs and truths. According to the core of his theory of hegemony, which gained renewed influence in contemporary critical political theory through its central place in Laclau and Mouffe's *Hegemony and Socialist Strategy*, hegemonic power expresses itself in subtle, almost invisible ways, embedded in what people take for granted. Or put differently: An order becomes hegemonic when its core ideas become common sense. Chantal Mouffe recently revisited this idea in her analysis of how neoliberalism persisted well beyond Thatcher's time in office. She notes that, by the 1990s in Britain, the central vision of neoliberalism "had become so deeply ingrained in the common sense that, when Labour came back to power in 1997 with Tony Blair, it did not even try to challenge the neoliberal hegemony."[40]

The same applies for scientific truths, methodologies, and belief systems, as Michel Foucault demonstrated through his analysis of

---

40   Mouffe, *For a Left Populism*, 32.

the epistemic orders that structure discourse: To analyze them as discursive orders means recognizing them as products of stabilized power relations. Gramsci and Foucault share the idea that these structures are most powerful when they are no longer seen as questionable—when their basic assumptions are simply taken for granted. But that is rarely the case. In most instances, we are dealing with a tangled landscape of competing discourses and counterdiscourses. In the framework developed by Laclau and Mouffe, these are seen as rival hegemonic projects.[41]

To understand how hegemonies endure, Gramsci's notion of common sense is key: Beliefs treated as self-evident are usually never questioned, precisely because they are perceived as such. Any serious critical reflection on standards must therefore cut through this invisible shield around hegemonic "truths"—exposing how the most "natural" beliefs, or those considered to be a matter of "common sense," are often rooted in power. And here is the crucial point: This kind of critique cannot happen within the accepted frameworks of scientific or political responsibility—because it needs to reach beyond them.

Not every discourse that goes beyond or challenges the status quo is emancipatory. The growing attacks on liberal democracy—from right-wing populists to the far right—are also counterdiscourses. They often include critiques of science, but these are usually based on conspiracy theories. And those theories only gain traction because they avoid critical examination altogether. There is no democratic or emancipatory core to be found in these movements, especially when they openly align themselves with far-right actors. Hence acting counterhegemonically is not, in itself, democratic or liberating. And simply challenging the existing order cannot justify one's actions, despite what many on the right claim—especially when they involve violence or hatred. Still, that does not mean we cannot draw lines between critiques that are democratic in nature and those that are not. To conclude, I want to outline two key tasks of a critical political theory that continues to embrace democratic skepticism about truth.

---

41   See Laclau and Mouffe, *Hegemony and Socialist Strategy.*

As I elaborated earlier, such a theory cannot situate itself within the framework of scientific objectivity as modeled on the natural sciences. Instead, it must question the very models of knowledge, concepts of truth, and evaluative standards—precisely because it must examine how all of these are tied to hegemonic social orders.

This brings us to the first task such a theory can take on, especially in the context of natural crises and the threats posed by related phenomena such as pandemics: It serves as a critical companion to current developments, decisions, and standards. It questions what seems self-evident and shows how such beliefs are the political results of successful hegemonic projects. But at the same time, it must also turn its critique inward. To be truly critical, it must also subject its own assumptions and its own actions to scrutiny. That is one of the clearest differences between such a theory and the conspiracy movements that resonate in today's right-wing politics. These movements often loudly present themselves as a critical opposition of righteous resisters and brave truth-tellers, but the fact that they are nothing of the sort is already evident in their refusal to question either themselves or their own standards. On the contrary, they deliberately place themselves beyond critique by claiming access to higher truths. Whether it is the supposedly superior knowledge that claims to expose hidden connections, or the aggressively and xenophobically asserted so-called rights of an ethnonationally defined people—in every case, they appeal to reference points that are themselves no longer open to questioning. Moreover, these challenges from the right are made in the name of rights that are meant to exclude others—while the critical perspective I pursue here challenges power imbalances in principle, not to defend privileges or exclusions.

If the first task is to critically expose what is taken for granted—revealing its entanglement with power and stripping away its veneer of self-evidence—then the second task, as already suggested above, is diagnostic: It focuses on the effects of these power imbalances.

Media and political discussions have rightly pointed out that the consequences of natural crises exacerbate existing social inequalities. Countries in the Global South and marginalized populations in the Global North tend to suffer far more from climate change or pandemics. And while, as Hegel once said of philosophy, "the owl of Minerva begins its flight only with the onset of dusk,"[42] we can still track unfolding patterns critically. In the case of natural crises, it takes no clairvoyance to see that they will intensify structural asymmetries and the injustices that result. The chapters that follow will explore the possibilities for critical reflection across various areas. With that, the diagnostic project of interrogating the present is linked to the possibility of democratic transformation—at the very least ex negativo, through the critical acts of questioning and inquiry.

---

42   Hegel, *Elements of the Philosophy of Right*, 23.

4. Neoliberal Hegemony? The Politics of Necessity and the Rise of Right-Wing Populism

Until recently, leading political theorists and philosophers—starting with Jacques Rancière and Colin Crouch and soon echoed more broadly[1]—were diagnosing the condition of contemporary politics using terms such as postdemocracy and postpolitics. But today's sharp divisions in political discourse across Western democracies seem to be moving beyond the idea of postpolitics, signaling a renewed return to political confrontation. At the same time, authoritarian populist movements are laying claim to a redemocratization of politics, with the suggestion that they are restoring the people's voice after its silencing by the elites in power.[2] It might well be argued that the political and structural constellation that has defined the last several decades is beginning to crack. Nancy Fraser describes this moment as an interregnum, a transitional phase with an uncertain

---

1   Crouch and Rancière each introduced the idea of postdemocracy independently. See Jacques Rancière's *Disagreement* and Colin Crouch's *Post-
     democracy*. This analysis has since been taken up by numerous others,
     including Slavoj Žižek in *The Ticklish Subject*, Chantal Mouffe in works such
     as *On the Political, Agonistics*, and *For a Left Populism*, and Ingolfur Blühdorn
     in *Simulative Demokratie*. On the concept of postpolitical, see Žižek's *The
     Ticklish Subject*, 198–205, and Mouffe's *On the Political*. In analytical terms,
     the idea of postpolitics—the disappearance of meaningful political debate
     over real social alternatives—is already embedded in the concept of
     postdemocracy.

2   Müller, *What is Populism?*

outcome. Using the United States as an example, she contends that there remains real potential for a new kind of left-wing politics, despite the surge of right-wing populism that brought Trump into office.[3] Chantal Mouffe makes a similar case, identifying a "crisis of the neoliberal hegemonic formation," while suggesting that such a moment opens space "for the construction of a more democratic order."[4]

At present, it must be acknowledged that, on one hand, the rise of right-wing populist movements has been much more successful than efforts to revive left-democratic projects. On the other hand, neoliberal hegemony—and the postpolitical condition it sustains—may prove far more resilient than Fraser's or Mouffe's crisis narratives would have us believe. While I agree with Fraser and Mouffe that neoliberal hegemony is now in crisis, this crisis has often ended up fueling right-wing movements—albeit ones that tap into the neoliberal ideal of negative freedom, giving it, as Wendy Brown powerfully argues, an authoritarian twist.

Brown asks a question that goes to the heart of our political moment:

> How has freedom become the calling card and the energy of a formation so manifestly unemancipatory, indeed routinely characterized as heralding "illiberal democracy" in its attacks on equal rights, civil liberties, Constitutionalism, and basic norms of tolerance and inclusion, and in its affirmations of white nationalism, strong statism, and authoritarian leaders?[5]

Her answer lies in what she calls authoritarian freedom—a vision of freedom that is allowing today's right-wing movements to build on neoliberalism's legacy. This does not mean, she underscores, that neoliberals such as Hayek have actively supported or endorsed far-right movements and their assaults on "immigrants, Muslims,

---

3   Fraser, "From Progressive Neoliberalism to Reactionary Populism."

4   Mouffe, *For a Left Populism*, 1.

5   Brown, "Neoliberalism's Frankenstein: Authoritarian Freedom in Twenty-First Century 'Democracies,'" 61.

Blacks, Jews, queers and women."[6] But the antigovernment, negative, and individualist concept of freedom advanced by figures such as Hayek and Friedman has become something right-wing parties and movements can easily adopt.[7] For Brown, the key point is that these right-wing trends "are in part effects of neoliberal reason."[8] Indeed, we can see how Trump's attacks on Obamacare during his first term, along with populist outrage at policies to foster gender equality or resistance to climate action in his second term, all draw on a rhetoric of freedom grounded in the neoliberal rejection of state regulation. What we are seeing, then, is less a break with neoliberalism than a shift within it—a transformation of neoliberal politics that, as Brown puts it, allows right-wing movements and their authoritarian brand of freedom to emerge as neoliberalism's monster.[9]

But if we want to understand the risks and opportunities of this current moment of crisis, it seems essential to grasp the continuity between two conditions: on one hand, the postpolitical and postdemocratic constellation described above; and on the other, the apparent repoliticization that has primarily empowered authoritarian forces on the right. That is the task of this chapter: to trace the depoliticizing and dedemocratizing effects of neoliberal hegemony and show how those dynamics have ultimately helped right-wing populist movements in their project to capture the language of democracy in the service of exclusion, discrimination, and racism.

Jacques Rancière offers one of the most radical and thought-provoking accounts of postdemocracy. His argument is so radical because democracy, in his view, is not simply a method for organizing political decisions; it is the very possibility of politics itself,[10]

---

6   Brown, "Neoliberalism's Frankenstein," 67.

7   See also von Hayek, *The Constitution of Liberty*; Friedman, *Capitalism and Freedom*.

8   Brown, "Neoliberalism's Frankenstein," 67.

9   Brown, "Neoliberalism's Frankenstein," 67.

10   See Rancière, *Hatred of Democracy*, 37–38.

and thus also the possibility of shaping the world.[11] This profound understanding of democracy and politics stems from the analysis of contingency discussed in Chapter 3—something Rancière shares, despite major differences, with thinkers such as Claude Lefort and Chantal Mouffe:[12]

> The foundation of politics is not in fact more a matter of convention than of nature: it is the lack of foundation, the sheer contingency of any social order. Politics exists simply because no social order is based on nature, no divine law regulates human society.[13]

Democracy is what Rancière calls this world-making, which is always a remaking, since we never encounter an unformed world, but always one already shaped by a particular police order. It is the shaping of a world without a given foundation for doing so,[14] and that is precisely what makes emancipation possible; it gives democracy its inherently contentious nature. Because the world's order lacks a fixed foundation, he argues—any *archē*—it can be disputed, allowing those who have been excluded to demand a share in shaping it.

Crucially, and this is where Rancière differs from a thinker such as Mouffe, the world does not need to be marked by a political ontology of conflict; such a view, he argues, would essentialize antagonism.[15] It is enough that the order of the world, being a historical product, is not rooted in any higher—natural or divine—authority. That alone opens the door to conflict and

---

11   See Rancière, *Disagreement*, Chapter 2. Rancière brings democracy and politics together conceptually; for him, both are practices that question and disrupt established (police) orders.

12   For an overview of differing concepts of the political in Lefort, Rancière, and Mouffe, see Oliver Flügel-Martinsen, *Befragungen des Politischen*, chap. 3.1.

13   Rancière, *Disagreement*, 16.

14   See Rancière, *Hatred of Democracy*, 37–38.

15   For a more detailed discussion of the differences between Mouffe und Rancière, see Flügel-Martinsen, *Befragungen des Politischen*, Chapter 3.1.

transformation. When the existing order—what Rancière calls the police order—is successfully challenged, it dissolves and is reconfigured. On this view, politics and democracy persist only so long as such disruptions remain possible. From Rancière's post-Marxist perspective, there can be no final resolution of politics—no arrival at a fully emancipated society where struggle ends. Any order, once contested, can be dismantled and rebuilt. This is why he is suspicious of the idea—put forward by Marxism and certain elements in Marx's writings (though others are also to be found[16])—that the communist revolution and the transition from the realm of necessity to the realm of freedom would bring an end to struggles over emancipation.[17] For Rancière, the idea—found in parts of Marx's work—that a truly free society would emerge when "the countenance of the social life-process, i.e. the process of material production ... becomes production by freely associated men, and stands under their conscious and planned control,"[18] implies that political struggle would no longer be necessary, thus insulating the resulting order from any critical interrogation. Even if such an order could not completely silence dissent, it would attempt to do so, and in doing so, reveal itself not as emancipatory but as a police order trying to prevent attempts to emancipatory politics.

Although political interrogation can never be permanently suspended, I do not believe this leads us to a broad ontological claim about the world's contingency. Rather, it is enough to see that existing orders can be undone and remade when challenged, because they

---

16   On this point, see Flügel-Martinsen, "Fehlt Marx eine Theorie des Politischen?"

17   On the transition from the realm of necessity to the realm of freedom, see Marx, *Capital: A Critique of Political Economy*. Volume III, 958–959. For Rancière's skepticism on the possibility that struggles over emancipation might come to an end, see Rancière, *Disagreement*, 82–88. Here, Rancière's thinking converges with Ernesto Laclau's, who speaks not of emancipation in the singular, but of emancipations in the plural; see Ernesto Laclau, *Emancipation(s)*.

18   Marx, *Capital I*, 173.

have no enduring guarantee, no secure anchor in any higher normative order. Any new distribution of the world—even one claiming to
be universally liberating—can, at any moment, itself be challenged
by those who have been excluded to have no or only an insufficient
part. The postrevolutionary history of human and civil rights provides a clear example in this regard. Even though the *Déclaration des
droits de l'homme et du citoyen* promotes a universal vision of rights, in
reality, it initially only applied to White men. This prompted Olympe
de Gouges to write her own counterpart, the *Déclaration des droits de la
femme et de la citoyenne*.[19] And slaves in Haiti were inspired by the *Déclaration des droits de l'homme et du citoyen* to fight for their freedom and
to launch a revolution. Yet de Gouges was beheaded during the revolution and remained largely forgotten until the twentieth century;
the revolution in Haiti, meanwhile, was long pushed to the margins
of Eurocentric historiography and histories of ideas. Rancière, for
his part, defines human rights as "the opening of an interval for political subjectivization,"[20] in other words, as a possibility for reshaping
the world that can be inserted into the existing order.

Rancière uses the term "postdemocracy" to describe a police order that has become hegemonic, to use a Gramscian concept refined
by Laclau and Mouffe for modern political theory.[21] Postdemocracy
thus defined immunizes itself against critique by presenting itself
as the self-evident and necessary order of things. In his analysis
of our present, Rancière argues that for postdemocracy to take
hold marginalize the *demos*, it also needs to marginalize politics:
"To evacuate the demos, postdemocracy has to evacuate politics,
using the pincers of economic necessity and juridical rule."[22] This
postdemocratic policing order can do so, he argues, because it

---

19   For the original French text, see de Gouges, "Les Droits de la Femme," and
      for the English translation de Gouges, "The Declaration of the Rights of
      Woman."
20   Rancière, "Who Is the Subject of the Rights of Man?," 304.
21   For Gramsci's concept, see Hoare and Smith, *Selections from the Prison
      Notebooks of Antonio Gramsci*, 329. On Laclau and Mouffe's reformulation,
      see, *Hegemony and Socialist Strategy*.
22   Rancière, *Disagreement*, 110.

convincingly claims that it is doing nothing but what is strictly necessary—that is simply following the demands of a world economy growing ever more entangled.[23] Politics in this sense forecloses any debate about its shape, because the language of necessity eliminates the idea that it could be shaped at all—that is to say, that people could choose between alternatives or argue over competing visions. If a certain kind politics leads to such an outcome, then we can call it hegemonic in the sense that its claims are no longer recognized as political at all but instead, as Gramsci would say, appear to be simple common sense.[24]

In *Les temps modernes*,[25] Rancière reconstructed this strategy—which becomes nearly invisible when it succeeds—and subjects it to a relentless critical interrogation. He approaches the idea of "the end of grand narratives" with several decades of historical distance,[26] focusing especially on the disappearance of the Marxist narrative of a historical future that once promised justice. The key point in his critique is that bidding adieu to this narrative of liberation did not, as the dominant tropes after the fall of the Iron Curtain would have us believe, signal the end of all meaning-making narratives. Instead, another grand narrative quietly took its place, proving remarkably effective. That narrative is the neoliberal one: of global markets, globalization, and its supposed lack of alternatives. It is this story, in his account, that underwrites both the birth of postdemocracy and the neoliberal politics of necessity. Historical necessity did not vanish, in other words; it simply changed shape. It no longer looks like the Marxist vision of a coming communist utopia. Now, it appears as the historical inevitability of a global free market—one that must not and cannot be subjective to any political governance:

---

23   Rancière, *Disagreement*, 112.

24   See Hoare and Smith, *Selections from the Prison Notebooks of Antonio Gramsci*, 247–248.

25   This text is part of Rancière's essay collection by the same title. See Rancière, *Les temps modernes.*

26   Rancière, *Modern Times*, 2. The phrase itself comes from Jean-François Lyotard.

Historical necessity received a new name. It was now called globalization. And globalization still seemed to involve a time determined by its immanent end, which was no longer revolution, but the triumph of global free market.[27]

Rancière's critique helps us clearly see that what is often called the politics of necessity—drawn from the narrative of the globalized free market—is itself a political order, even if it tries to disguise itself as something else and insists it is not political at all. To use Rancière's terminology, it functions as a *police order*—an arrangement that seeks to appear inevitable, natural, and spontaneous, so as to mask the fact that it has been, and continues to be, actively produced through specific strategies, such as neoliberal deregulation and privatization.

To understand the neoliberal police order that remain dominant today, despite ongoing challenges from protest movements, it is helpful to consider Wendy Brown's analysis, drawing on Michel Foucault, of the rationality underlying neoliberal governance:

> In contrast with an understanding of neoliberalism as a set of state policies, a phase of capitalism, or an ideology that set loose the market to restore profitability for a capitalist class, I join Michel Foucault and others in conceiving neoliberalism as an order of normative reason that, when it becomes ascendant, takes shape as a governing rationality extending a specific formulation of economic values, practices, and metrics to every dimension of human life.[28]

Reading neoliberalism not just as a set of governing *policies*, but—as Brown puts it—as a governing *rationality* helps us grasp it not simply as a package of political strategies, but as a normative framework that shapes decisions and rules while penetrating every corner of social and political life. The idea of governance that comes into view here goes well beyond a narrow understanding of government that is confined to formal political institutions. When Foucault—and

---

27   See Rancière, *Modern Times*, 12.
28   Wendy Brown, *Undoing the Demos*, 30.

4. Neoliberal Hegemony?   63

Brown, following him—speak of the government of the living,[29] both are referring to complex webs of power and means by which people are shaped as subjects across diverse areas of social life. As Foucault writes:

> Basically, power is less a confrontation between two adversaries or the linking of one to the other than a question of government. This word must be allowed the very broad meaning which it had in the sixteenth century. "Government" did not refer only to political structures or to the management of states; rather, it designated the way in which the conduct of individuals or of groups might be directed: the government of children, of souls, of communities, of families, of the sick.[30]

In discussions about neoliberal governmentality, the term is usually not employed to mean politics or state bureaucracy; such notions are not even its main focus. Instead, it is used in reference to a broad range of domains pertaining to everyday life. For neoliberal rationality to become the dominant discourse, it must establish itself as hegemonic within a network of power dynamics and relations; it must, as Gramsci would put it, become common sense. And if we follow Foucault in tracing how discursive formations emerge from both discourses and counterdiscourses, we can also see why even dominant discourses are never entirely immune to challenge, and how they can, in fact, be questioned and transformed.

The key to such challenges lies in alternative forms of sub-jectivity—precisely the kind of subject formation at odds with dominant power structures that Foucault saw in the early LGBT movement in the United States.[31] The concept of subjectivation is

---

29 Michel Foucault, *On the Government of the Living*.

30 Michel Foucault, "The Subject and the Power," 789–790.

31 At present, Judith Butler's work is especially noteworthy in advancing these ideas. For my own exploration of the theory of resistant subjectiva-tion, see Flügel-Martinsen, "Subjektivation: Zwischen Unterwerfung und Handlungsmacht und Macht zwischen Unterwerfung und Widerstand"; the discussion there also includes extensive references to relevant writings by Foucault and Butler.

thus inherently double-edged. On one hand, it describes how we become subjects under dominant discourses; on the other, it also signals the possibility of resisting that process, through a break from subject-formation and the creation of new ways of becoming a subject. It is no accident, then, that Foucault uses the French term for subjection—*assujettissement*—to underscore the tension within subjectivation between subordination and resistance.[32] Foucault sees these ideas—a point that is crucial to the argument of this essay—as a form of critical analysis of the present moment. Regarding the intention of such interrogation, he in unequivocal: "Maybe the target nowadays is not to discover what we are but to refuse what we are."[33]

Understanding the stability of an order such as neoliberal discourse, requires—as I have suggested above—other theoretical tools in addition to those developed by Foucault in his work. Gramsci's idea of hegemony, for instance, helps explain why essentially contingent orders can still hold firm: Hegemonic power works by turning particular viewpoints into what feels like self-evident, everyday truth. Discourses become stable, then, when they are hegemonic to the point that their core assumptions seem natural and unassailable within everyday life. To make sense of this stability and persistence, Rancière's insight remains key: that we are not simply dealing with "power relationships" ("rapports de pouvoir") but rather with "relationships between worlds" ("rapport de mondes"),[34] as each order constitutes a kind of world-making. Still, as we already saw above (in Chapter 2), such world orders can be disrupted—set into motion—by questions that expose their

---

32   See, for example, expressions such as "mode d'assujettissement" (mode of subjection) in Foucault, *Histoire de la sexualité* 2, 34, or "procédures d'assujettissement" (procedures of subjection) in Foucault, *L'ordre du discours*, 46. I have discussed this two-sided character of subjectivation at length elsewhere: see Flügel-Martinsen, "Zwischen Unterwerfung und Handlungsmacht."

33   Foucault, *The Subject and the Power*, 785.

34   Both quotations are from Rancière, *Mésentente*, 67 (English: *Disagreement*, 42).

contingent nature. A contesting of this order can also fail—or remain stalled for quite some time—depending on how deeply the hegemony has taken root, that is to say, how deeply its core beliefs and standards have embedded themselves into what people take for granted.

Neoliberal rationality has enjoyed incredible success over the past few decades. Its core claim—that governance must be for the market, because the market, as Foucault puts it, is the "site of veridiction,"[35] that is to say, the place where truth reveals itself (or does not)—has permeated the very warp and weft of our contemporary societies. This is evident on the level of politics in the way the neoliberal logic has become more than a partisan agenda. It could be argued this was the case about neoliberalism in the early 1980s, when such a project became state policy under Ronald Reagan in the US and Margaret Thatcher in the UK. But since then, it has also taken hold in the opposing camp. Nancy Fraser points out that, in the US, the Democrats' progressive identity politics under President Bill Clinton entered into a strategic alliance with neoliberalism, an arrangement she calls progressive neoliberalism.[36] Chantal Mouffe draws similar conclusions about the UK, showing that Thatcher's neoliberal hegemony was so strong that it became the guiding doctrine of New Labour under Tony Blair, even long after she left office, ultimately shaping both major political parties in the country.[37] Looking at German politics from around the turn of the millennium to the end of Angela Merkel's term, one telling sign is the use of the language of necessity, an idea that justified both the reforms in the early aughts to social and labor policy under Gerhard Schröder and the austerity policies that Merkel championed at the European level during the financial and currency crisis.

In all of these cases, the market served as the site of veridiction, to use Foucault's terminology, because the effectiveness of political decisions was judged first and foremost by how well they aligned with market logic (e.g., the demands of the global market), not by other

---

35   Foucault, *The Birth of Biopolitics*, 33.

36   See Fraser, "From Progressive Neoliberalism to Reactionary Populism."

37   See Mouffe, *For a Left Populism*, 32.

standards such as social equity or equal opportunity. Other values of this kind may have been cited for political legitimation, but there was never any room for serious doubt about the supremacy of market demands in a globalized context. That this era has been—and still is—a time of rapidly increasing wealth inequality and concentration in Western democracies only underscores this dynamic. Neoliberal rationality's view of the market as the site of veridiction leads, in concert with other political benchmarks, to a deeply paradoxical situation: In a neoliberal order, politics must govern *for* the market. That means the market must be actively supported and even made possible through political action. This stands in stark contrast to classical and neoclassical economic liberalism, where, following Adam Smith's famous notion of the invisible hand, the market is seen as a self-regulating system whose "natural" forces balance things out—so long as it is left alone.[38] Neoliberalism flips this state of affairs: It demands that governments *govern for the market*, yet strictly forbids them from *governing the market*. Time and again, one can see the consequences of this contradiction playing out in political life. Perhaps the clearest indication is that governments are judged by how well the economy performs. They are, in effect, held hostage by the ups and downs of the global market, which is seen as the only legitimate judge of policy, even as they have neither power nor justification to take its helm or guide its course. At the same time—to repeat the point made above, along with its postdemocratic implications—they are required to submit to market exigencies. That is the essence of governing for the market.

Examining neoliberalism not merely as the political agenda of specific political currents but as a normative order makes it possible to understand why neoliberal policy has become not just the platform of a particular political faction, but the hallmark of centrist governance—toward which both the conservative-bourgeois and the left-progressive camps, and thus most political parties, have moved over the past two decades. It also clarifies

---

38   Wendy Brown explores these distinctions between classical liberalism and neoliberalism in her dialogue with Foucault. See Brown, *Undoing the Demos*, *Chapter II*.

why this framework has come to permeate all spheres of social life: The normative order of neoliberalism now profoundly shapes even commonplace reasoning. This explains, as Brown emphasizes, why its influence[39]—and indeed its formative power—extends far beyond the realm of monetization: Neoliberal economics manifests itself by imposing a logic of marketization and market-based comparison, even in domains where money is not at issue. To give a concrete example: The neoliberal transformation of universities, which Brown examines with reference to the United States,[40] is happening within the German university system, as well, even though private universities and exorbitant tuition fees play no more than a marginal role in Germany. One is tempted to argue this is simply a consequence of declining baseline funding for German universities, which increases the pressure to operate with an entrepreneurial logic and to compete for research grants on a third-party funding market.[41] This overtly monetized mode of neoliberal economization is undoubtedly a component of the neoliberal restructuring of Germany's academic landscape. However, if neoliberalism is understood, following Brown, in the significantly broader sense of a normative order, then a different set of phenomena and transformations comes into view: German universities are being neoliberalized, like those in the United States, in that their academic programs are being subjected to market-based comparison through rankings, or research quality is being assessed not by content, but by metrics supporting comparisons based on market-like logics. More explicitly monetized criteria for assessment, such as the measurement of scholarly excellence by the volume of third-party funding acquired, undeniably play an important part here. Yet equally significant is the fact that the logic of economization extends into the structuring of fields that are not monetary in nature.

We might then also ask: To what extent does neoliberal hegemony foster the success of populist movements, especially on

---

39   See Brown, *Undoing the Demos* , 31

40   See Brown, *Undoing the Demos*, Chapter VI.

41   See Münch, *Academic Capitalism.*

the authoritarian, right-wing? The liberal mainstream of political philosophy and theory long neglected this development, but the work of authors such as Chantal Mouffe and Jacques Rancière has long offered powerful insight here. Both thinkers have addressed the resurgence of nationalist and authoritarian political movements across numerous Western democracies that had only begun when they were writing, but which has now been realized to an alarming degree. Both connect their reflections on reactivating an emancipatory concept of democracy based in left-wing politics with a forceful critique of consensus- and necessity-driven political reasoning. We have already discussed how Mouffe and Rancière regard a politics that suppresses the possibility of fundamental dissent in the name of consensus and necessity to be as an abandonment of democratic agency. Rancière famously refers to this as postdemocracy;[42] Mouffe supplements this diagnosis with the concept of postpolitics.[43] In my analysis, these diagnoses are based on divergent ontological understandings of the political—or of politics more broadly. Mouffe insists on the ontologically antagonistic character of the political. Rancière, by contrast, appears to assume only the contingency of every police order and does not offer a strong argument that the political space is ontologically conflictual. However, when viewed in light of the explanatory power their respective critical diagnoses hold—which is the primary focus here—this divergence is ultimately negligible. For that reason, I will not pursue it further at this point.[44]

The neoliberal politics of consensus and necessity thus effectively suspends politics itself, insofar as it forecloses dissenting counterspeech. But how, then, is this connected to the successes of nationalist and racist politics? As early as 2005, Mouffe pointed out—with reference to empirical examples—that right-wing populist parties tend to gain traction especially when mainstream political parties converge toward a centrist consensus, leaving voters

---

42   See Rancière, *Disagreement*, Chapter 5.

43   See Mouffe, *On the Political*, Chapter 4.

44   For a detailed discussion of these differences and their implications, see Flügel-Martinsen, *Befragungen des Politischen*, Teil 3, especially Chapter 3.1 and 3.4.

without any real alternatives. She refers to the rise of the FPÖ in Austria in the late 1990s and the Vlaams Blok in Belgium in the early 2000s. It is under such conditions, she notes, that right-wing populist movements succeed in presenting themselves as the alternative.[45] They do so by injecting suppressed political conflict back into public discourse, using anti-immigrant scapegoating to reestablish antagonism.[46] Seen this way, neoliberal consensus politics offers right-wing populist actors a strategic opening to stage themselves as democratic alternatives. It is no coincidence that German right-wing populism adopted the name Alternative for Germany and portrays itself as a victim of an oppressive dictatorship of opinion.

Rancière, too, sees the politics of consensus and necessity as a major driver behind the return of racism and anti-immigrant sentiment. He was arguing as early as the mid–1990s—well before the resurgence of right-wing populism in many Western democracies—that the disappearance of the worker as a political figure had left it divided:[47] The worker had now come to appear as either a White racist, or as an immigrant as one who is foreign, Other, and ultimately turned into a target of hostility. In this constellation, the dispossessed have lost their subject position as the proletariat and now appear divided into two opposing camps: as migrants vs. new racists.

Following Rancière, we can diagnose a key dynamic of our time: The disappearance of a category historically tied to emancipatory struggles has created a fracture in the political discourse—one that leaves the neoliberal "police order" of necessity intact. As I suggested above: Right-wing populist reinterpretations of globalization

---

45   See Mouffe, *On the Political*, Chapter 4.

46   This is why Mouffe is now explicitly takes sides, presenting her stance as a political intervention aimed at countering the nationalist and racist critique of consensus politics through a left populist strategy. This strategy seeks to reactivate democratic dissent under a new banner and to open up a left-wing, emancipatory perspective on democratic practice, rather than ceding democratic rhetoric to the right. See Mouffe, *For a Left Populism*, 9.

47   See Rancière, *Disagreement*, 117–118.

do not alter the unequal distribution of wealth and income in a deregulated economy. Instead, they turn one group of those affected—migrants—into a scapegoat, while pitting them against another vulnerable group—low-skilled workers and those in the lower-middle-class who are anxious about losing ground. That split remains central to understanding right-wing populist success even more than twenty years later. The case of Donald Trump is especially telling: The rise of his reactionary populism,[48] which has now brought him a second White House term after the Biden interruption, can be explained, as Nancy Fraser suggests, by the failure of the political left to represent the interests and identity of economically disadvantaged groups.

Still, a core question remains: Why has the success accrued to the right and not to the left? Why has the right managed to brand itself as an alternative, while the left has failed to offer a comparably broad-based challenge to the centrist neoliberal consensus across Western democracies? One answer was suggested earlier in this chapter with Wendy Brown's idea of an authoritarian understanding of freedom: Right-wing movements are able to tap into neoliberal rationality and its negative conception of freedom—particularly when they frame efforts to bring about equality as oppressive state overreach. This is clearly the strategy of the far-right AfD in Germany, which leverages an authoritarianized version of negative liberty to stir up opposition not only to a politics of gender diversity but also to climate policy. During the coronavirus pandemic, the AfD tried to energize a protest movement against public health measures—a movement shot through with far-right extremism. These new right-wing movements, which in recent years have weakened democratic norms and institutions—and in some cases gained governmental power—are able to appropriate neoliberal language and give it an authoritarian spin. That gives them a structural edge over left-wing movements, which, in the face of a crisis of neoliberal hegemony, must first establish, or reestablish, alternative ideas of freedom, such as a more social conception. The transformations of gender politics add another dimension here: With global reach, right-

---

48   See Fraser, "From Progressive Neoliberalism to Reactionary Populism."

authoritarian parties have successfully targeted men, portraying them as victims of supposedly antimale, feminist policies of gender equality, with the result that they have garnered many male votes. Although structural gender inequality persists despite some progress, the right's narrative that men are being increasingly disadvantaged has proven extremely effective. Sociologist Steffen Mau, for example, has shown how gender dynamics play a key role in parts of eastern Germany where the far-right AfD performs especially well—and how the AfD deliberately speaks to those dynamics.[49] Trump's renewed push for the presidency followed a similar playbook, appealing to men with sexist narratives explicitly opposed to gender equality. He not only retained massive support from White male voters but also made surprising inroads among men from groups that traditionally lean Democratic, such as Black Americans. Politics against trans people and the recognition of gender diversity add another important and very violent dimension of today's right-wing movements in many countries, as Judith Butler has recently underlined once again.[50]

In addition, the broader context of global inequality and economic globalization—which will be discussed below (see Chapter 6)—further erodes the ground on which left-wing projects might take root. That is why I believe the prospects for populist projects on the left like those Mouffe envisions are limited.[51] In fact, I see a very real risk that these so-called left-wing initiatives may, whether unintentionally or through strategic neglect, begin to resemble right-wing ones. This danger is evident in the renationalizing rhetoric of figures such as Jean-Luc Mélenchon in France, who has gained widespread support while attacking the European Union as a whole and calling instead for a return to a strong, national welfare state—rather than working toward a left-wing, social transformation of the EU. We see something similar in Germany with the newly founded BSW (Bündnis Sahra Wagenknecht), a party that has adopted antimigrant talking points alarmingly

---

49   See Mau, *Ungleich vereint.*

50   See Butler, *Who's Afraid of Gender?*

51   See Mouffe, *For a Left Populism.*

close to those found in right-wing populist discourse. Mouffe acknowledges the risk that national identity might become a vehicle for nationalist politics if left unchallenged. But here, her call for a left-wing populism becomes strangely ambivalent. On the one hand, she seeks to eschew nationalism, arguing that the left-wing populist struggle for a radical, emancipatory democracy must, for tactical and strategic reasons, begin—but not end—at the level of the nation-state. She emphasizes, for instance, the need 'to establish an alliance at the European level.'"[52] On the other hand, some of her claims, such as "a left populist strategy cannot ignore the strong libidinal investment at work in national—or regional—forms of identification and it would be very risky to abandon this terrain to right-wing populism," are dangerously imprecise.[53] It remains unclear what a truly left-wing response to the affective pull of national identity might actually look like; and Mouffe, at least here, does not attempt to spell it out. Her suggestion that left strategies should draw on the egalitarian aspects of national discourse offers little practical guidance, given that right-wing parties are already doing precisely that. Right-wing movements benefit from the fact that national equality is often framed as the equality of a presumed homogeneous group—defined in opposition to "others," who are then denied equal rights by limiting access to egalitarian social rights to members of an imagined national community.

Moreover, the postwar nation-state model of the welfare state—which managed for a time to mollify the conflict between labor and capital and establish a measure of social justice in Western democracies—is, in today's globalized economy, no longer a structurally viable strategy. Criticizing the EU as a whole also means overlooking the fact that its much larger scale—compared to individual member states—might in fact offer protection against the harshness of a globalized economy, if it were reshaped with a sense of solidarity instead of continuing in its current role as primarily a market-based alliance.

---

52   Mouffe, *For a Left Populism*, 71.

53   Mouffe, *For a Left Populism*, 71.

In my view, there is good reason to doubt whether renational-ization strategies can be called leftist projects at all—despite claims from certain left-wing populists, whose positions dangerously echo those of the far right—especially given today's extreme global inequalities. Right-wing populists are particularly good at ignoring this second issue, since they cast those trying to improve their lives through migration—amid intolerable global inequality—as villains, and call for the ruthless defense of privileges based on national belonging that are already falling apart. There is a real danger that this hostility toward migrants, often racist and marked by a reckless push for easy answers, is helping to drive the rise of right-wing populism, while left-wing politics, in a world marked by staggering inequality, seem to have lost any emancipatory vision. Trying to recover or reinvent a guiding vision for the left purely through theory seems, to me, to miss the importance of political action and, in turn, to overstate the role theory can play within those struggles. But that does not mean theory has no voice. It can still help interrogate the now frighteningly successful language and identity politics of the right and take on the task of critically analyzing the social and political conditions we face today. That is the focus of the next two chapters—first on the persistence and return of exclusionary politics (Chapter 5), and then on the issue of borders and global injustice (Chapter 6).

.

5. The Ongoing and Renewed Rise of Essentialist Politics of Exclusion: Essentialist Strategies for Excluding the Other

If we look closely at today's politics, the landscape feels haunted. The very ideas we thought we had left behind—views that surged in the nineteenth century and culminated in the horrors of the twentieth—appearing to be creeping back: aggressive nationalism, chauvinistic assertions of identity and presumed superiority, and racist exclusion. We should not confuse the present with the past, but history can certainly help us understand what we are seeing today. That includes contemporary ways of thinking about group identity and the Others they define—and often reject.

And if we consider how philosophers and theorists have approached the relationship between group identity and its Other, we might feel reminded of Paul Klee's *Angelus Novus*, as Walter Benjamin famously described the painting.[1] Benjamin sees this figure as the angel of history, staring at the past—once likened by Hegel to a "slaughter-bench"[2]—with eyes wide open to the horror and devastation it beholds. Likewise, the intellectual tradition reflecting on the relationship between constructions of collective identities and the Others they demarcate reveals genuine abysses in the history of thought—chasms with starkly real counterparts in the historical practices of violence by which these exclusions have been

---

1   See Benjamin, "On the Concept of History," 392.

2   Hegel, *The Philosophy of History*, 35.

made. When one examines these dynamics, it is not the collective self-aggrandizement of collectives or their discriminatory and violent exclusions of the Other that appear anomalous and in need of explanation, but the exceptions to these practices. The basic patterns here were already established in antiquity and have since reappeared in forms tailored to each historical context. In Aristotle, for instance, we encounter key internal and external figures serving to exclude the Other, such as the distinctions between Greek and barbarian,[3] free man and slave,[4] or man and woman.[5] To be sure, distinctions are, in principle, epistemically foundational: Self-identities—like all entities—become visible and come into being only through processes of differentiation. Distinctions, then, are not inherently problematic; they open up conceptual space and produce a diverse world by giving rise to difference. What is problematic, as numerous texts from the history of ideas show, is that hardly any distinction exists that does not simultaneously elevate one side and devalue the other. Jacques Derrida inscribed this point emphatically into the philosophical tradition with his deconstructive interrogation. As he demonstrated, what may initially seem like purely epistemic distinctions are often bound up with power relations that function to assign value or devalue. These mechanisms help stabilize—or even produce—the dominance of the privileged side over its Other.[6] Critical inquiry into these repressive modes of constructing the Other plays a pivotal role—as found, for instance, in both Judith Butler's gender theory[7] and in postcolonial discourse.[8]

Intoxicated by the apparent triumph of history, liberal discourse in the late twentieth century largely lost sight of the persistence of such distinctions, and the exclusions they perpetuate. But they continued to fester beneath the surface: As the previous

---

3   See Aristotele, *Politics*, 1252b.

4   See Aristotele, *Politics*, 1252b.

5   See Aristoteles, *Politics*, 1252a.

6   See Derrida, "Tympan."

7   See Butler, *Gender Trouble*.

8   See, for instance, Spivak, "Can the Subaltern Speak"; Said, *Orientalism*; Hall, "The West and the Rest."

chapter showed in analyzing the rise of right-wing populist parties and movements, thinkers such as Jacques Rancière and Chantal Mouffe—at still marginal at the time in many areas of political theory and philosophy—were warning, as we discussed above in Chapter 4, even in the 1990s and early 2000s that the dominance of liberal consensus and its discourse in Western-style representative democracies would open the door to the return of right-wing nationalist positions, which could present themselves as viable alternatives to liberal hegemony.[9] That is exactly what is happening today—with alarming success.

And along with these right-wing positions, chauvinist claims to identity and racist tropes of exclusion have once again become entrenched and visible parts of public political discourse. Indeed, in several EU countries they have even become part of government agendas. When such willful rejection of emotional restraint is performed in parliaments or government offices—or, as during both of Donald Trump's terms, becomes the signature style of a sitting U.S. president's online communication—there is little to stop it from spreading further into society. So it is hardly surprising that sociologists now speak of regressive trends of "decivilization" in Western societies.[10]

One of the most potent constructions of collective identity currently fueling calls to exclude the Other is the idea of "the people" as a clearly bounded national collective. At a time when right-wing populist movements loudly invoke national values and cultural identity as goods to be defended, and as firm reference points for a shared identity vis-à-vis imagined Others, it is crucial to reiterate that these are nothing more than fantasies. Yet such fantasies are increasingly motivating rhetorical threats of violence in political discourse—especially across multimedia platforms—and

---

9   See Rancière, *Disagreement*; Mouffe, *The Democratic Paradox*.

10   See Nachtwey, "Decivilization: On Regressive Tendencies in Western Societies." The very notion of "civilization," however, is itself part of an exclusionary logic, one that draws a boundary between the civilized West and the uncivilized rest, thus laying the normative groundwork for colonial exploitation and domination. See Hall, "The West and the Rest," 308.

these, in turn, are helping to drive a marked rise in violent crimes against dissenters and migrants.[11] No normative justification can be articulated for such acts, which right-wing populists and extremists have recently tried to romanticize as "resistance."

Viewed in light of the history of ideas, the modern notion of a sovereign people has always been an open and indeterminate category. The historical emergence of "the people" as a democratically self-governing and thus sovereign collective is—as Claude Lefort's reflections on democracy and the political (discussed in Chapter 3) make clear[12]—bound up with a specific experience of contingency: For Lefort, the democratic age is one in which fixed points of orientation dissolve. Seen thus, democracy is a response to the recognition that the world we inhabit must be made and shaped, and is not simply given in the form of a stable and normatively binding order.[13] The locus of power—most starkly expressed through the physical and symbolic decapitation of the monarchy during the French Revolution—is, in democratic modernity, "empty" in the sense that it can only ever be temporarily occupied, and that every occupation is open to contestation.[14] With the experience of lost certainty and the emptiness of power's place comes an inevitable contingency of that collective known as the people, for its identity, too, is no longer anchored in fixed reference points.

The inverse of this process is the recurring temptation to reconstitute this now fundamentally fragmented and pluralized collective identity as a unified body of the people. While radical democratic thought views the pluralization and indeterminacy of popular identity as an opportunity to justify and redefine democracy, this is often met with reactive efforts to restore certainty—sometimes

---

11   See "Beratungsstellen registrieren Zunahme rechter Gewalt in Ostdeutsch-land," https://www.zeit.de/gesellschaft/zeitgeschehen/2019-04/rechtsextr emismus-gewalt-berlin-ostdeutschland-zunahme.

12   See Lefort, *Democracy and Political Theory*. For recent work on Lefort's political theory, see Oppelt, *Gefährliche Freiheit: Rousseau, Lefort und die Ursprünge der radikalen Demokratie*.

13   See Lefort, "La dissolution des repères et l'enjeu démocratique."

14   See Lefort, "Démocratie et avènement d'un 'lieu vide.'"

through force—by imposing a fixed political and cultural identity. Democratic modernity's foundational experience of contingency thus provokes a persistent discomfort with uncertainty, fueling repeated attempts to escape its grasp. Lefort, writing in the twentieth century, was thinking above all about the allure held by imagining the people as a unified collective—a fantasy that underpins totalitarian efforts to bypass the contingency inherent in democracy. Yet it is not difficult to interpret today's right-wing nationalist revivals as symptoms of the same diagnosis: They, too, aim to impose a stable unity precisely where democratic plurality keeps reopening the question of who or what the people actually is.

If Lefort's insights into the breakdown of stable points of orientation are taken seriously, then the desire to found a collective unity must ultimately prove groundless. And because that is the case—and because persistent plurality takes the place of the unity being sought—any effort to forge a singular identity of "the people" can only proceed through violence: They will find no pregiven unity, but can only resort to coercive acts that construct identity by excluding the Other. Yet because the Other is unavoidably embedded in any construction of the people as a shifting, multifaceted body, such efforts to enforce a collective identity always entail acts of exclusion—and, in extreme cases, of violent annihilation. It is no coincidence that nationalist projects incite violence against those who visibly embody the ongoing and irreducible transformation of a democratically constitute "people," not least those who demand that they belong. Following Jacques Rancière's reflections on political subjectivation,[15] we see that this struggle over who counts as the people in a democratic sense is shaped above all by those who, in a given historical moment, exist as the "part with no part" (*la part des sans-part*)—those who enter into a political struggle for "a redistribution of the places, the identities, and the parts."[16] A common thread runs from the fight of the workers' movement's for political participation, to feminist struggles for equal rights and current efforts by migrants to gain a voice in the political decision-

---

15   See Rancière, "Politique, identification, subjectivation," 112–125.
16   See Rancière, "Critical Questions on the Theory of Recognition," 90.

making of the societies where they live and work, even though often
lack full political rights: It is the formation of collective identities
through exclusion, and the possibility of challenging these identities
by exposing their contingency. Rancière insists on this contingency
just as forcefully as Lefort, and it plays a decisive role in his theory of
the political battles waged by those who have been excluded from the
polis, since it is precisely the contingent nature of political (policing)
orders and the understandings of collective identity they support
that makes them open to being questioned by anyone—*n'importe qui*.
In Rancière's terms, democratic political conflict over how the world
is organized is only possible because collective identities—and
the structures that uphold them—are contingent through and
through.[17]

This kind of contestation presupposes, of course, the insight that
categories such as "people" or "nation" are themselves contingent.
Here, Derrida's strategy of deconstructive interrogation offers
crucial clues, which lead us to this chapter's central critical thesis:
That the idea of a self-identical people is, in the end, nothing more
than a fantasy. As Derrida shows in *Politics of Friendship*, the gestures
that nationalist narratives employ to fix categories of identity and
collective belonging can be easily destabilized once it becomes clear
that their appeal to supposedly solid foundations—such as shared
descent—is ultimately grounded in imagined constructs. These are
fictions, however, that have horrifying real-world consequences—of
exclusion, violence, and in some cases annihilation—for those cast
as the Other to this imagined and renaturalized community. What
matters most for Derrida, however, is that these exclusions can be
challenged:

> All politics and all policies, all political discourses on "birth," mis-
> use what can in this regard be only a belief: some will say: what
> can only remain a belief; others: what can only tend towards an
> act of faith. Everything in political discourse that appeals to birth,
> to nature or to the nation—indeed, to nations or to the universal

---

17   See Rancière, *Disagreement*, 16.

nation of human brotherhood—this entire familialism consists in a renaturalization of this "fiction."[18]

Keeping these reflections in mind, we can draw a sharp distinction between right-wing populist movements that try to forge a collective identity by excluding others—often through violence—and democratic struggles for political participation, which always already acknowledge the diversity and malleability of the people's collective identity. In Rancière's account of political subjectivation—where those he calls the part with no part (la part des sans-part) claim a place—what is at stake is a remaking of the political stage and the distribution of positions upon it, aiming to broaden the political collective rather than close it up through exclusionary mechanisms.[19] Some years ago, Judith Butler reminded us that protests in the name of the people are central to democratic politics, yet the people themselves can never be fully assembled or represented, since every attempt to do so triggers conflict about who or what the people actually are.[20] Building on Lefort, Rancière, and Butler, we can say that democratic protest and the democratic making of a people depend on staying mindful that democratic identity is inherently open to contestation over its meaning and its boundaries. Right-wing populist movements, in contrast, claim to be the people in a single sense—or at least to speak for the people without question. It can thus be said that they instrumentalize the language of democracy while being fundamentally antidemocratic, because they reject pluralism.[21]

---

18   Derrida, Politics of Friendship, 93.

19   For more on political subjectivation, see Flügel-Martinsen, Befragungen des Politischen, Chapter 3.3.

20   See Butler, "We the People" – Thoughts on Freedom of Assembly," 155–156.

21   See Müller, What is Populism? Unlike Müller, who, in my view, does not draw a clear enough line between left- and right-wing populism, I believe it is essential to highlight that right-wing populist movements in particular build collective identities through radical antipluralism and xenophobia. Even where Müller explicitly discusses left-wing populism, I do not think he seriously considers this crucial distinction.

As we have seen, the notion of national identity is deeply problematic in all its forms—not just the most extreme one—and has recently made a disturbing comeback in politics. In new right-wing discourse, it often becomes fused with other exclusionary ideas. In many cases, these crude configurations—built from exclusionary tropes wrongly thought to be long behind us—manage to pass as the new political normal because they attract disturbing levels of electoral support, enabling them to shift the broader political discourse to the right.[22] They use cunning tactics of reinvention, as seen in the ways that contemporary racism often appears in the guise of cultural racism. Biologistic racism—which developed out of anthropological theories of race from the eighteenth century,[23] and which served in the nineteenth and twentieth centuries (often underpinned by social Darwinist ideas[24]) as the basis for White domination, oppression, and exclusion—is now receding. The theories of race on which it has been built have been exposed as scientifically untenable, not least by deconstructions based in biology. The exclusion and oppression of the groups it once targeted continues today—now in the form of cultural racism. As Thomas McCarthy notes, the social construction of racism thus remains stable even when scientific theories change:

> Since the structures of domination and exploitation embodied in differences of economic role, social standing, political power, and the like could be maintained across changes in scientific theories of race—in a self-reinforcing feedback loop with "common-sense" racist beliefs and practices—the disappearance of scientifically

---

22   See Welzer, "Die Rückkehr der Menschenfeindlichkeit." on how discourse has shifted to the right in Germany.

23   In the German-speaking world, Immanuel Kant and Johann Gottfried Herder both developed influential theories of race as part of their anthropological thinking. See Immanuel Kant, "On the Different Races of Human Men"; Johann Gottfried Herder, *Ideas for the Philosophy of the History of Humanity*. On Kant's racial thought, see also Thomas McCarthy, *Race, Empire, and the Idea of Human Development*, Chapters 2 and 3.

24   See McCarthy, *Race, Empire, and the Idea of Human Development*, Chapter 3.

certified races did not bring an end to racial stratification. Just as postcolonial neoimperialism could outlive the demise of formal colonies, post-biological neoracism could survive the demise of scientific racism.[25]

It is this combination of the insidious and overt persistence of exclusionary and oppressive practices—rooted in long-lasting stereotypes that, as Gramsci would say, are hegemonically embedded in everyday common sense—that is driving the success of right-wing populist politics in today's North Atlantic societies. When parties like the AfD in Germany, the Rassemblement National (until recently known as the Front National) in France, the Fratelli d'Italia and the Lega in Italy, or the FPÖ in Austria bring Islamophobic and racist politics from the street into formal political institutions, it is due in large part to their ability to draw on a long-standing tradition of racist and culturalist exclusion and devaluation, in which different discriminatory traditions converge. These traditions in fact only appeared to disappear—and, as we are currently witnessing, can be reactivated without difficulty. Discourses of national, cultural, and racial superiority come together to form an aggressively anti-immigration political agenda. Ideas such as the "superiority of the West"—imagined as a civilized, Christian world facing off against a more or less savage remainder—and degrading tropes such as an Orient allegedly incapable of reaching, or even threatening, the cultural achievements of the Occident, reflect a long-standing Western tradition of considering itself to be superior, as highlighted in the work of Stuart Hall and Edward Said.[26] And as today's discourses hostile to migration, driven by the populist right, make clear, these tropes can easily be revived for current political use.

Often, it takes nothing more than a single incident for these stereotypical patterns of exclusion to spread from the far right into sectors of society that usually regard themselves as the political center or even the center-left. Such was the case with the highly publicized and hotly debated sexual assaults on women that

25   McCarthy, *Race, Empire, and the Idea of Human Development*, 6–7.

26   See Hall, "The West and the Rest," and Said, *Orientalism*.

occurred near the Cologne train station and Cathedral Square on New Year's Eve 2015–2016, reportedly carried out by individuals with migration backgrounds. These events led to the rapid spread of a rhetorical style and symbolic repertoire that had, until then, been largely confined to the populist and extreme right but now suddenly appeared across broader media coverage. As documented by the leftwing newspaper *taz*, images of black hands reaching for white female bodies were featured not only in the news magazine *Focus*, but also in the *Süddeutsche Zeitung*, a newspaper generally considered a flagship publication of the liberal middle class.[27] Regardless of who made up the group of perpetrators in this specific case, what occurred was a general uptake and use of racist stereotypes in public debate—stereotypes with a long and damaging history in the record of racial discrimination. Images and symbols of unrestrained, threatening sexuality have long played a role, not only in twentieth-century American racism, but also in the antisemitic propaganda of the Nazi movement. In particular in the dynamic between the (Christian) West and the (Islamic) Orient, this binary coding has played a foundational role, both in how these social constructions came about and in how they have been sustained: "The Oriental," Edward Said notes, "is irrational, depraved (fallen), childlike, 'different'; thus the European is rational, virtuous, mature, 'normal.'"[28]

This image—of female innocence under threat from the racialized "Other"—is central to many right-wing populist campaigns. It produces what may, at first glance, seem like a contradictory rhetorical fusion in the discourse of the populist right. On the one hand, many on the right are outspoken defenders of patriarchal structures of power, which imply broad control over women's sexuality. Yet in the Cologne case and its aftermath, they attempt to latch onto the language of defending women's rights. Even though this transparently opportunistic appropriation of feminist rhetoric is, unfortunately, at times reinforced by feminists such

---

27   See Sander and Böcker, "Titel der Schande," See also Weissenburger, "Deutschland postcolognial."

28   Said, *Orientalism*, 40.

as Alice Schwarzer, the strategy itself is easy to see through. It functions entirely within the patriarchal logic of "protecting" women—women who are understood as property, inaccessible to "foreigners" or the "Other," while the patriarchal man, so to speak, grants protection while nevertheless retaining sexual access. Such a logic is, moreover, to be secured through a rigid gender order. The coexistence of discourse against gender diversity and the supposed defense of women's rights in right-wing populism is, then, only seemingly contradictory. On closer inspection, it fits seamlessly into the consistent logic of a patriarchal system that is not only sexist but also racist.[29] Regrettably, it is necessary to acknowledge that such arguments have been rendered socially acceptable in part by statements made by former leaders of the women's rights movement. In the exchange between Sabine Hark and Judith Butler on one side, and Alice Schwarzer on the other, for instance, it became clear that Schwarzer not only affirms the Orientalist and racist prejudices of right-wing populists but even embraces the gender essentialism that serves as the pseudo-intellectual foundation of right-wing discourse against "gender."[30]

A theory based in an interrogative critique of politics and the political may not be able to dismantle these powerful exclusionary discourses on its own. But its method of deconstructive needling—of continuous and insistent questioning—can help counteract their consolidation by refusing to accept the essentialist narratives upon which they are built. This is by no means a mere academic exercise. It can in fact provide powerful tools in the field of political struggle. What is needed, then, is for disciplines such as political science to regain the confidence to engage in such normatively critical interventions—interventions that go far beyond the narrowly professionalized collection of facts under the guise of science.

---

29   For an overview of this position, see Hark and Villa, *The Future of Difference: Beyond Toxic Entanglement of Racism, Sexism, and Feminism*.

30   See also the relevant contributions in *Die ZEIT* by Judith Butler and Sabine Hark, and by Alice Schwarzer: Butler, Hark, "Die Verleumdung"; Schwarzer, "Der Rufmord."

In this context, Judith Butler's work has, for many years now, stood as one of the most significant and effective forms of theoretical intervention in the political sphere. Having spent the 1990s developing the conceptual tools necessary to deconstruct gender essentialism[31]—and racism[32]—Butler deserves recognition in their later work for drawing out the implications of these ideas for political theory. In doing so, they have challenged the patterns by which conventional, racist narratives about perpetrators reverse the actual threats within these discourses; their tactic has been to rethink these dynamics through the lens of precarious, endangered life.[33] Human life, in its mortal form in vulnerable body, is necessarily exposed to the risk of injury. Yet Butler's concern is not to propose an anthropology of vulnerability and finitude as a *conditio humana*. Rather—and this is where their work gains its critical edge—they are interested in the radically unequal distribution of such vulnerability. It goes without saying that we all must die, and that we are all susceptible to injury and illness over the course of our lives. But the fact that the chances for a long, healthy, and secure life are so unequally distributed—and that this disparity cannot be explained by "natural" chance but must be traced back to political and social conditions—carries the seeds of a critical diagnosis of our times. It is precisely this critique that Butler places at the center of their concept of precarity:

> "Precarity" designates that politically induced condition in which certain populations suffer from failing social and economic networks of support more than others, and become differentially exposed to injury, violence and death. As I mentioned earlier, precarity is thus the differential distribution of precariousness. Populations that are differently exposed suffer heightened risk

---

31   See Butler, *Gender Trouble*.

32   See Butler, *Excitable Speech*.

33   See Butler, *Precarious Life*; Butler, *Frames of War*; Butler, *Notes Toward a Performative Theory of Assembly*.

of disease, poverty, starvation, displacement, and vulnerability to violence without adequate protection or redress.[34]

This uneven distribution of vulnerability goes back to various forms of exclusion and deprivation. In addition to racist and sexist exclusion, we must also consider the socioeconomic precariousness tied to class structures, something brought into sharp focus in Édouard Louis's literary portrayals of his own life. In vivid, often brutal imagery, Louis documents the physical toll taken on his family, who live in the working-class regions of northern France. While this issue appears more as a subplot in his debut novel *The End of Eddy*,[35] which primarily centers on his experiences growing up gay in the hypermasculine, rough environment of rural France, it takes center stage in a later book. That, later work reads as a fierce critique of the French class system and the political machinery that maintains it:[36] In *Who Killed My Father*, Louis tells his father's story as one marked by injuries resulting from class-based instability and vulnerability. These bodily scars are framed as an emblem of a broader political point—highlighting, as Judith Butler does, how political systems heighten the risk of vulnerability: "The history of your body stands as an *accusation* against political history,"[37] Louis writes of his father. Louis gives a far more sympathetic portrayal of his relationship with his father here than in his earlier work, where his father was the face of a homophobic, patriarchal, small-town culture rooted in harsh, White masculinity. Over time, the father begins to change. He opens up—perhaps inspired by his son's life and writings—and starts to shed some of the racist and homophobic beliefs he once took for granted. Still, as Louis stresses at the end, his father's damaged body ultimately prevents him from fully becoming the person he might have been: "But because of what they've done to

---

34   Butler, "Gender Politics and the Right to Appear," 33.

35   Louis, *The End of Eddy*.

36   Louis, *Who Killed My Father*.

37   Louis, *Who Killed My Father*, 85–86, emphasis in the original.

your body, you will never have a chance to uncover the person you've become."[38]

The recent surge of right-wing populism suggests that the transformation Louis sees in his father is, unfortunately, likely the exception rather than the rule. More typical is the pattern Didier Éribon describes in his own family, who also come from the French working class. They moved away from their historically leftist roots in the Communist Party and began supporting the Front National,[39] now the Rassemblement National. The structure underlying this kind of political shift has been widely noted in commentary on the populist right: After the political left failed to deliver on its promises—and in fact played a part in deepening economic insecurity—many working-class and even downwardly-mobile middle-class voters turned to right-wing populists. These movements offer an anti-immigrant message, promising to "reclaim" the welfare state by closing borders and enforcing racist policies, granting its benefits only to an imagined ethnic-national community.

The images offered by Louis and Éribon are grim. Louis's father—physically broken and denied the chance to live in any different way—is, in Éribon's analysis, the exception. For what seems to be more typical, judging by the success of right-wing populists in Western democracies, is that one precarious group turns against others who are likewise—and often even more severely—vulnerable. Nevertheless, Judith Butler rightly insists that even in the face of such bleakness, precariousness can be a form of resistance. Bodies are vulnerable—and it is precisely for this reason that they can publicly confront, and expose, systems of violence.[40] When bodies put themselves at risk in the streets, they create powerful images and spaces—especially when amplified by the media—that can have major political impact. But let us be clear: The embodied performativity of this resistance often suffers injury or even death. Those who face the weapons of the repressive state—or the violent

---

38   Louis, *Who Killed My Father*, 86–87

39   See Éribon, *Returning to Reims*.

40   See Judith Butler, "Bodies in Alliance and the Politics of the Street," 83.

mob of a far-right march—armed only with the vulnerable openness of their own body, may be wounded or even killed.

And it is precisely when subjects in performative acts of resistance take on this very risk that their performance makes it possible to create a subversive space of appearance—one that can challenge and potentially topple the established order. When vulnerable bodies appear and persist in public space, they generate a counterdiscourse—one both material and symbolic—that derives its force from the bare fact that these bodies can be harmed, disfigured, or destroyed. Literary accounts of bodies broken and permanently scarred by exploitative labor, such as *Who Killed My Father* by Édouard Louis, also form part of a broader political and social struggle against domination, violence, and exploitation.

As valuable as Butler's thoughts on resistance are—for making room for counterdiscourses and challenging disempowering narratives of victimization—it must be acknowledged that, for many people, visible resistance remains out of reach. These individuals remain, to a large degree, the often overlooked victims of a global order marked by extreme inequality. Oppression, exploitation, and precarity affect different groups in different ways, leading to complex forms of conflict. Today, for example, we can see that those in OECD countries who experience precarious conditions are especially drawn to populist promises. These promises drive desires to support parties and movements that target their hostility at the oppressed and exploited in the Global South—at those hoping, under the pressure of a global economy, for a livable future in the North Atlantic world. This multifaceted precariousness can only be understood within the larger framework of a world marked by borders and structural inequality. The book's final chapter now turns its focus to that world.

6. A World of Borders and the Suppressed Issue of Global Injustice

Discussions of borders and global injustice are deeply and structurally intertwined.[1] Yet when we look at today's public debates across the OECD countries, that connection is easy to miss. Border talk is everywhere—especially as right-wing populist movements gain momentum—and the spotlight has increasingly turned toward securing frontiers. This discourse about border security, rendered ever more dominant by the rhetorical shift to the right, works deliberately to obscure, or outright deny, the structural link between border politics and global injustice. This discourse presents each country as responsible for its own people, imagined as one, homogeneous national unit, which requires it to strictly limit or at least regulate border crossings. Migration for socioeconomic reasons is denied any legitimacy at all. The fact that these forms of labor and poverty migration are rooted in structural patterns of

---

1   Here and in what follows, I will refer to global injustice, rather than global justice, contrary to the dominant language of mainstream international political theory. I do so, first, to emphasize that injustice—not justice—defines our current reality, and second, to suggest that theories of justice might be better approached as theories of injustice. Why I believe a theory of injustice is preferable to a theory of justice will become clear later (see the section below entitled "A Call for Critical Interrogation and Critique of the Present in International Political Theory"). Though still in the minority, attempts to build such a theory can be found in twentieth-century and contemporary justice debates. See Flügel-Martinsen and Martinsen, *Ungerechtigkeit*.

global inequality and exploitation is intentionally elided. And the narrative of denial and defense against "Others" encroaching into the nation continues to easily gain purchase because the political left, though partly aware of the connection, ultimately offers no real response.

As early as the nineteenth century, Hegel noted in his *Philosophy of Right* that within society, "hardship at once assumes the form of a wrong inflicted on this or that class."[2] According to Iris Marion Young, we already live in a state of global social interconnection,[3] meaning that global inequalities, following Hegel's diagnosis of the impoverishment experienced by certain classes within bourgeois society, must be understood not merely as unfortunate differences but as a manifestation of global injustice. But alongside the view that social impoverishment constitutes injustice, Hegel also offers a second, more skeptical thesis: that the wealth of bourgeois societies is not sufficient "to prevent an excess of poverty and the formation of a rabble."[4] On a global scale, this second thesis seems to have become an almost universally accepted diagnosis. Today, left-wing parties and movements are marked by a deep internal tension—between those who advocate cosmopolitan policies of open borders and those who seem convinced that, without a renewed focus on the model of redistributive welfare based in the nation-state, they risk losing supporters en masse to the political right. Whether the nation-state perspective even counts as a leftist option in a globalized world is highly questionable, especially given how this focus on national redistribution tends to ignore global injustice, as well as the global climate crisis, which individual nation-states are hardly equipped to address.

What is clear today is that the tacit consensus spanning from center-right to center-left since the 1990s, which treats the free global market as the conditio sine qua non of politics and yardstick for political reform, has played directly into the hands of right-wing

---

2   Hegel, *Elements of the Philosophy of Right*, § 244. Addition.
3   Young supports this view by pointing to the complex web of connections that shape global society. See Young, *Responsibility and Global Justice*.
4   Hegel, *Elements of the Philosophy of Right*, § 245.

populists. Faced with the bleak choice between this neoliberal consensus and the right's slogan of *fellow citizens first*, the left remains paralyzed. This chapter will not attempt to formulate a political program that offers a way out of this deadlock. That is the responsibility of political engagement and debate within democratic society. The contribution of theory, by contrast, lies in critical interrogation and diagnosis—and especially in bringing to light connections that are all too often pushed aside in public debate, such as the link between border discourses and global injustice. Political theory must seek out a form allowing it to meet this critical task in a world structured by borders and vast inequality.

The dominant liberal approach to international political theory, as it currently stands, is based on a deeply inadequate understanding of what political theory is. I will thus begin turning to the case of liberal-cosmopolitan border discourse to show how damaging it is when the political constitution of subjects and systems is excluded from the outset. In a second step, I will outline possible starting points for a theoretical perspective that takes this political dimension seriously, allowing it to make a substantial contribution to a critical interrogation of our present. I will also examine why the urgent questions of global injustice are being pushed out of public discourse in today's OECD societies.

Political, Not Moral: On the Critique of Liberal Common Sense in International Political Theory

Political philosophy and theory have been rooted for centuries in the framework of the nation-state, which has meant that normative questions were almost always conceived in terms of societies structured by the nation-state model. Though this has gradually begun to shift over the past few decades—with international political theory gaining ground for its ability to look beyond the narrow confines of this framework—the nation-state perspective still often holds a privileged conceptual and epistemological status in much of this more recent discourse. We can see the dominance of the nation-state model especially clearly in the influence of John

Rawls's work on debates about global justice. Rawls developed his theory of justice squarely within the context of nation-state societies,[5] and his later attempt to address global issues beyond the nation-state remains a significantly scaled-down version of that theory, subordinate to the original national framework.[6]

But even in cases where political theory breaks away from the nation-state as its default frame, this does not automatically mean it takes political power relations seriously. The recent surge in philosophical debate about borders makes this especially clear, as most of these discussions explicitly bracket out the real conditions of global political life. In doing so, they overlook the concrete political realities of a world shaped by borders—an issue to which we will return shortly. In today's tightly interconnected debates on borders and global justice, political theory seems stuck in a false choice between particularist and cosmopolitan positions. Particularist approaches maintain the normative and epistemic primacy of nation-state-based communities by grounding their reflections on justice in the framework of the nation-state (or similar specific collectives), and by granting these collectives normative priority.[7] Cosmopolitan perspectives, by contrast, place their thinking beyond the nation-state, but in doing so, they systematically disregard the *political* contexts of global society in the strict sense. Avoiding a consideration of how communities and subjects are constituted within multilayered and deeply entangled power relations, they instead posit a liberal subject abstracted from all such conditions, to then reflect on its moral rights and duties[8]—rights and duties that are then transferred wholesale into the political sphere without further mediation.[9]

---

5   See Rawls, *A Theory of Justice*.

6   See Rawls, *The Law of Peoples*.

7   See Miller, "Reasonable Partiality Toward Compatriots."

8   See Carens, "Aliens and Citizens: The Case for Open Borders."

9   See also Raymond Geuss's sharply polemical critique of this entire paradigm of political philosophy as a form of applied moral theory: *Philosophy and Real Politics*.

The problematic trend of approaching political theory from a moral-philosophical standpoint—and thus abstracting away from its distinctly *political* dimensions—is especially evident in the long-running philosophical debate over borders. This debate, which has become more urgent in light of recent surges in migration and refugee movements, is now widely seen as one of the most pressing issues of our time, far beyond the confines of academic theory. A rigorous treatment of this topic—one that makes the problems of a moral-philosophical approach to political theory particularly clear—can be found in Andreas Cassee's study on global freedom of movement.[10] In his book, Cassee adopts a line of argument that cuts against the grain of both the political and philosophical mainstream by making the case for open borders. As Cassee himself observes, the standard position "undoubtedly holds that states are justified—not only legally but also morally—in refusing entry or long-term residence to those wishing to immigrate" (21).[11]

To challenge this widely held view and defend open borders, Cassee swiftly turns to a moral-philosophical argument centered on individual freedom of movement. Ultimately, he reinforces this position by adapting Rawls's contract theory, but in a way that runs counter to Rawls's own conclusions. In short, Cassee concludes that, pace Rawls,[12] global justice should begin not with states but with individuals—and that, in the original position, these individuals

---

10   See Cassee, *Globale Bewegungsfreiheit*. In what follows, I develop my critique of liberal cosmopolitanism—which assumes a conception of personal autonomy as prior to politics—through a close reading of Cassee's argument. I have chosen this focused, exemplary approach over a broad summary, as it allows for a more detailed discussion of specific problems and objections. That said, I believe the critique laid out here can, in its core thrust, also be extended to other liberal approaches to the border debate—most notably the position put forward by Joseph Carens. See Carens, "Aliens and Citizens: The Case for Open Borders."

11   The German passages from Cassee's book have been translated into English. Page references to the book appear in parentheses throughout the text.

12   See John Rawls, *Law of Peoples*.

would agree on the right to freedom of movement as one of the basic liberties.

Cassee has without question produced a careful and well-reasoned moral-philosophical analysis of a highly important issue. His book is, moreover, a powerful and at times eye-opening accomplishment, one that systematically subjects long-held assumptions to such sustained and critical scrutiny that they begin to lose their air of inevitability. But from the standpoint of political theory and philosophy, the unavoidable question is whether a moral-philosophical perspective is even the right way to approach the issue at hand. For several reasons, I do not believe it is. Even though Cassee positions himself outside the mainstream currents of moral philosophy, he still follows a now widespread—and deeply problematic—trend in practical philosophy, closely tied to Rawls: the tendency to treat political philosophy through the lens and methods of moral philosophy.

It is truly striking—especially with a subject like national borders—to find a theory that so thoroughly overlooks their fundamentally political nature and treats politics as nothing more than an offshoot or zone of application for moral theory. Political theory, as an approach of its own, does not even register as a serious option in Cassee's framing of the inquiry; from the outset, he takes the moral-theoretical approach as a given, treating politics as if it stood on equal footing with positive law. This likely explains why he moves straight from noting that "immigration restrictions ... are legal" (15) to asking whether "states (or their citizens) have a *moral* right to restrict immigration to their territory" (15).

Cassee's decision to adopt a moral-philosophical perspective from the very beginning shapes the entire structure of his book. His analysis asks what rights *moral* subjects can claim—and in doing so, takes those subjects to be *prepolitical* by default. This rich tradition of social and political philosophy—from Hegel, Marx, and Nietzsche, to figures as varied as Adorno, Foucault, Rancière, Butler, and Honneth—that insists on understanding norms and subjectivities as socially and politically formed, is pushed aside in favor of an essentially ahistorical view of normativity and the subject. In Cassee's moral-philosophical framework, subjects are historically situated only in a superficial sense: that they live within certain legal-political contexts. But these contexts appear merely external to the autonomous subject, whose validity is judged from a moral standpoint that floats above time and place. This division is also evident in Cassee's work, as in many similar approaches, following Rawls's well-known distinction between ideal and nonideal theory. Fundamental issues are dealt with morally, within ideal theory, while political concerns surface only in nonideal theory, where they are treated as secondary, practical applications. The roles are clearly divided: Normative issues are treated as matters of moral philosophy, while politics is relegated to the realm of nonideal, factual arrangements. The notion that political normativity could exist in its own right—neither a mirror of legal-political facts nor reducible to a moral point of view—no longer even enters the picture.

As noted, this is not a move unique to Cassee's work. His study is representative of a broader trend in contemporary philosophy: the tendency to approach political theory through the lens of analytic moral philosophy, which has largely severed its crucial connection to the interpretive social sciences, leaving them to serve only as a kind of appendix with the task of adjusting reality. An approach of this sort ignores a path that has proven fruitful since Hegel—against Kant's abstract moralism—to wit, a sociological perspective on normativity and subjectivity that treats both as socially mediated, including individuals' normative self-conceptions and claims. That subjects not only exist within specific historical contexts but are actually produced within them—or as Foucault puts it, *subjectivated*—and that the normative frameworks they inhabit cannot be derived from any prediscursive idea of an autonomous subject, is something a moral-theoretical lens is fundamentally incapable of recognizing.[13]

Cassee engages a political-theoretical perspective only fit-fully—and even then, only in the context of considering a possible democratic objection to the standard view. Even at that point, it is evident how little weight he gives to the political dimension of the issue: He notes, almost in passing, that he must leave open the

---

13   I present a full critique of this type of political philosophy—and an alternative trajectory—in Flügel-Martinsen, *Befragungen des Politischen*.

question of "whether unilateral immigration restrictions imply a democratic deficit" (208), without suggesting this question has any real bearing on the rest of his argument. But even when this theoretical perspective on democracy is taken as the starting point—as in the explicitly democratic framework proposed by Arash Abizadeh—the criticism still holds: Politics and democracy remain external to the argument so long as the conceptual and normative core rests, as it does for Abizadeh, on a moral-philosophical conception of personal autonomy that posits individuals and their rights exist prior to any political domain or the political as such.[14] This downplays questions about how subject positions are formed—and how political institutions and orders are created or transformed—if not eliding them entirely.

If political theory is developed, by contrast, from within a broader social-theoretical perspective that aims to interrogate the present, the very questions that Cassee and most analytic-normative thinkers treat as marginal come to the fore. In this case, subjects and normative orders can no longer be treated as preceding the political and the social. Rather, we must ask: In what contexts are subjects constituted? How are they shaped by particular normative structures? And how are those structures themselves formed? These questions leave space to ask about the drawing of borders, but the question then shifts: It becomes a properly political issue rather than a moral one. There are many possible ways to approach this; here, I will simply sketch a perspective that shows how my own critically interrogative theory of the political might engage with the issue of borders.

Drawing on Rancière's ideas about the distribution of the sensible,[15] borders can be seen as one of the clearest manifestations—or sedimentations—of what he calls police orders. For Rancière, a police order refers to a system that organizes parts—how things and roles are allocated and justified—and assigns places to different groups accordingly. Rancière argues that police orders generate "those with no part": groups excluded from the existing order and

---

14   See Abizadeh, "Democratic Theory and Border Coercion," 39–42.

15   See Rancière, *Disagreement* and *The Politics of Aesthetics.*

its distributional logic, denied any place on the shared stage, and therefore barred from speaking, let alone participating in decisions about who receives what parts and who belongs where. It is no accident that Rancière, in his analyses of contemporary society, repeatedly points to migrants and refugees[16]—the *sans papiers* who remain, in especially stark ways, "those with no part."

This perspective also allows us to question the drawing of borders, and to do so through a political logic, without falling back on the problematic assumption of moral subjects that are positioned as prior to the political realm. What Cassee treats as a peripheral democratic concern becomes central here, and engaging it does not require any prior moral-theoretical assumptions. If we follow thinkers such as Foucault, Lefort, Butler, or Rancière in viewing our societies and political systems as contingent constructions, then, as Rancière puts it, their borders can be questioned by anyone (*n'importe qui*), because these orders—and their divisions—have no underlying structure that places them beyond challenge. Quite the opposite: Contesting borders becomes a fundamental act of political engagement.

This perspective, in contrast to a moral-theoretical approach to borders, is rooted in social theory; and crucially, it does not depend on any prepolitical normative category, such as the autonomous moral subject equipped with rights to liberty. In my view, then, this approach is more modest in its normative assumptions, while also being more deeply grounded in political and social reality. Whether or not one fully adopts this perspective, it highlights something crucial: A political-theoretical approach to borders changes the nature of the question itself. It shows that the moral-theoretical standpoint is not neutral, but belongs to a normative order that is itself contingent. Taking this even somewhat seriously compels us to consider what it means to say that there is no such thing as an independent, prepolitical standpoint of autonomous subjects—and how we might nevertheless address normative questions in political terms. The approach I have proposed—against the moral-philosophical framing of this issue—understands the act

---

16   See also, for example, Rancière, "Who Is the Subject of the Rights of Man?"

of contesting borders as a democratic practice of calling existing orders into question. Its politically normative power stems from one thing: demonstrating the contingency of these orders and the boundaries they draw, both within and without, because on this view, all political orders carry an element of arbitrariness—which is exactly what makes them contestable. A moral-philosophical approach to these issues—however well-intentioned, as in Cassee's case—inevitably obscures political and social dynamics by treating them as epiphenomena or secondary effects. As a result, theoretical reflection ultimately loses sight of the question of power, which is crucial for understanding normative issues, as Raymond Geuss emphasizes in *Philosophy and Real Politics*, his powerful polemic against the moral-philosophical narrowing of political philosophy.[17] In short: Borders are a political issue—and must be treated as such.

A Call for Critical Interrogation and Critique of the Present in International Political Theory

For any political theory that sees critical interrogation of the present as one of its central tasks, it is crucial—indeed unavoidable—to approach borders and global injustice in ways that differ from the typical methods of liberal, normative political philosophy, with its tendency to abstract away from social context and the dynamics of power. There is an alternative, at the margins of current debates in contemporary political theory: a genuinely *political* mode of thought that takes seriously how conflict and power relations constitutively shape subjects and orders, especially when analyses attempt to move beyond the limits of the nation-state. In Derrida's later writings, this kind of perspective is developed under the *topos* of a critique of sovereignty;[18] Rancière likewise dedicates a brief but significant essay to a way of thinking about the political that moves beyond the nation-state, and also beyond the prepolitical liberal subject that

17   See Geuss, *Philosophy and Real Politics*.
18   See Derrida, *Rogues*.

dominates mainstream normative political philosophy today.[19] His account of a political conception of human rights does not rise above a suggestion but has been more thoroughly elaborated in Franziska Martinsen's study on the borders and limits of human rights.[20] Finally, in the field of justice theory, the works of Iris Marion Young continue to offer rich insights into a political theory of injustice in global perspective.[21]

The shape of an international *political* theory that puts critical interrogation and contemporary analysis at its core can be sketched by critically examining two defense mechanisms that are key to understanding the political debates in today's OECD societies. The first deals with global injustice and might best be described as a resistance to assuming responsibility; the second involves a kind of fear-based denial, which can be seen as a reaction to changes in how access to wealth and work opportunities are globally organized. Since both topics involve complex issues, I will limit myself here to a few illustrative reflections. I will explore the issue of responsibility denial using Iris Marion Young's thoughts on global injustice; I will take up the fear-based response in a discussion of Achille Mbembe's thesis about a "tendency to universalize the Black condition."[22]

Denying Responsibility: The Repressed Question of Global Injustice

From the start, Iris Marion Young turns standard assumptions in theories of justice on their head—assumptions that still dominate much of today's discourse. Most theorists, as noted above, follow John Rawls in linking redistributive justice to the institutional and communal frameworks of societies based on nation-states. Young, by contrast, argues forcefully that such political and institutional forms of community should not be seen as the basis for claims of justice, but rather as responses to obligations that emerge from

---

19   See Rancière, "Who Is the Subject of the Rights of Man."

20   See Martinsen, *Grenzen der Menschenrechte*.

21   See Young, *Global Challenges*.

22   Mbembe, *Critique of Black Reason*, 4.

the standpoint of justice.[23] As discussed above, Rawls initially designed his theory of justice with societies based on nation-states in mind;[24] and in his later shift toward a postnational perspective, he emphasized that there are no obligations of justice at the global level comparable to the principles of redistribution that apply within nation-states.[25] This position—labeled "particularist" in the debate on global justice[26]—is defended in especially strong terms by David Miller, who argues that redistributive justice only becomes relevant in the context of what he sees as the unique bonds defining national communities.[27]

Young's theory of justice, by contrast, begins from a fundamentally different place: Her now-classic 1990 book *Justice and the Politics of Difference* criticizes the narrow concern of theories of justice with redistribution. In her view, the core issue in justice is oppression; unequal distribution is to be seen as a consequence of underlying structures of domination.[28]

Young thus approaches justice by critically interrogating existing systems of oppression and injustice.[29] This opens up an entirely different angle on the philosophical question of responsibility within justice theory: By starting, first, from a focus on oppression and exploitation and then treating these as structural phenomena, Young does not—like Rawls and many who follow him—center

---

23   See Young, "Responsibility, Social Connection, and Global Justice," 160.

24   See Rawls, *A Theory of Justice.*

25   See Rawls, *Law of Peoples.*

26   See also the key debate between particularist and cosmopolitan positions in Broszies and Hahn, *Globale Gerechtigkeit.*

27   See Miller, "Reasonable Partiality Toward Compatriots." Miller restates these claims in his later work on the philosophy of migration: Miller, *Strangers in Our Midst.* For a strong critique of this entire approach, see Celikates, "Weder gerecht noch realistisch—David Millers Plädoyer für das staatliche Recht auf Ausschluss."

28   See Young, *Justice and the Politics of Difference*, Chapter 1.

29   For one of the (rare) approaches that pursue justice theory ex negativo—from the standpoint of injustice—see Flügel-Martinsen and Martinsen, "Ungerechtigkeit," 53–59.

her account on the institutional conditions needed to form a redistributive collective.[30] Instead, she broadens the view to include all social relations that generate injustice. The result is a perspective on justice that goes far beyond the nation-state and entails a much broader definition of responsibility. From a standpoint concerned with theories of justice, all structures and processes that place people in relations capable of producing oppression or injustice are relevant. In Young's view, the question of justice, in a globalized world, crosses national borders from the outset.[31] And a structural approach to responsibility, oppression, and injustice changes how we understand who bears responsibility for what, and how oppression and injustice come about: Under an actor-centered model of responsibility, responsibility falls on those who actively cause harm—such as exploitation or oppression—to others through intentional action. But the situation looks very different when, as Young argues, responsibility—like injustice and oppression—is understood as a structural phenomenon. One example can help clarify the actor-centered concept. No one in Western Europe who regularly buys cheap clothing produced under exploitative conditions in the Global South necessarily has any intention of exploiting or oppressing someone. But from a structural point of view, it is not simply that some of us in the world are lucky and other are not. Everyone is part of a global exchange system marked by unjust, exploitative structures; and those who benefit from these unjust conditions share responsibility for those who are exploited, even if they have absolutely no intention of doing harm.

The view—frequently put forward by right-wing populist move-ments—that people from the Global South who come to the North in search of a better life are merely economic migrants—directly denies this context of theorizing justice and the questions it raises. According to this view, so-called economic migrants have no legitimate claims; citizens of privileged countries, it is said, owe them nothing. But if we take Young's arguments seriously, then such nationalist strategies of rejection construct national collectives

---

30   See Young, "Responsibility, Social Connection, and Global Justice," 168.

31   See Young, "Responsibility," 159.

that exclude the claims of others by denying the link between injustice and the responsibility that follows from it. This does not automatically determine what political consequences follow. A borderless world may be politically out of reach at the present time. What is clear, however, is that simply rejecting claims to have a part is not a legitimate option—and that the demands of those who have no part, in Rancière's sense, are more than just appeals to minimal humanitarian obligations, such as those recognized even by particularist positions.[32] These are demands for justice, because we are all part of a global system that generates both privilege and exploitation. There may be significant political and social barriers to addressing these structures of injustice comprehensively and without delay. Constructing a nationalist, narrowly defined community of solidarity may nevertheless succeed in excluding others and disowning responsibility. Yet contrary to what right-wing populists assert, this does not amount to a valid justification for doing so. Collective identities—introduced in nationalist discourse as self-evident or fixed points of reference—and the exclusionary practices tied to them, as we saw in detail in Chapter 5, cannot withstand critical interrogation. It also becomes clear that these ever-shifting collectives, whose members acquire citizenship rights through historically contingent processes, are embedded in structures relevant to theories of justice that extend well beyond any particular nation-state. There is good reason to suspect that right-wing populist actors are waging their exclusionary battles so fiercely today precisely because they have an inkling, however vague, of these larger connections. It is also quite plausible to assume that this dawning awareness—of global injustice and the arbitrariness of one's place within it—gives rise to fear. And in response to that fear, national identity is conjured up as a supposed normative right to exclude others. We will therefore now take a brief look at this defense mechanism driven by fear and the displacement of blame it entails.

---

32   See Miller, "Reasonable Partiality Toward Compatriots."

Fear-Based Defense and Shifting of Guilt and Obligation: "The tendency to Universalize the Black Condition"

In the previous section, the discussion of global injustice relied, without further interrogation, on the distinction between the Global North and the Global South, yet this distinction no longer appears fully adequate. While it still offers some orientation—as the global distribution of wealth and poverty generally allows us to distinguish between richer countries (mostly in the Global North, especially the so-called North Atlantic world) and poorer countries in the Global South—its limits are increasingly evident. The direction of current migration flows seems, at first glance, to confirm this global split. But the image of such sharply drawn lines is full of cracks—cracks that matter for understanding the recent resurgence of collective identities that define themselves by excluding others. We may think here of how opportunities to live a good life have been made precarious by the effects of a globalized neoliberal economy,[33] which no longer aligns cleanly with old global-geographic divisions. Instead of reinforcing those distinctions, today's economic situation is dismantling the so-called egalitarian middle-class societies in the Global North, and in their place, deepening inequalities and large segments of Western populations living in poverty—or at least under structurally precarious conditions.

Of course, it would be an oversimplification to say that those experiencing this precariousness are the primary base of support for right-wing populist movements and their success. But it is hard to deny that their existence—and the broader dangers of precarization, driven by neoliberal policy and economics—help fuel sentiments against migration. These are precisely the sentiments, moreover, that authoritarian populist actors exploit by shifting the blame for neoliberal precarization onto stigmatized Others. These stigmatized Others are said to threaten the national prosperity of Western countries, and their presence—so the argument goes—prevents citizens from accessing resources that right-wing

---

33   On this analysis of precariousness, see Nachtwey, *Germany's Hidden Crisis: Social Decline in the Heart of Europe.*

populists contend should be reserved exclusively for members of the national community. Nancy Fraser offers a stark and deliberately provocative framing of this complex situation in the title of one of her essays: In "From Progressive Neoliberalism to Reactionary Populism," she argues—through an analysis of Trump's victory in the 2016 U.S. presidential election—that the rise of a right-wing populist president cannot be understood without the neoliberal politics that came before.[34] By now, the structural effects of decades of neoliberalism have become so entrenched that even Biden's attempts to reverse them during his presidency have failed, enabling Trump to campaign successfully for a second term using right-authoritarian and anti-immigration rhetoric.

Fraser argues that the desire among voters to reject austerity, free trade, and poorly paid work also underlies other right-wing populist successes,[35] such as the Brexit referendum in the United Kingdom or the rise in influence of the Rassemblement National (formerly the Front National) in France. Right-wing populist parties and movements manage to redirect both fear and blame: Fear about slipping into a precarious situation is converted into fear of Others—others who are cast as outsiders by a conjured national collective. This goes hand in hand with a shift in those who are taken to be at blame: The main cause of precarization is no longer seen as the unleashed forces of neoliberalism, but instead as "foreigners" who, as right-wing populist narratives have it, must be excluded from the comparatively affluent, "comfortable" community of a national collective defined in nationalist and often racist terms. From this perspective, the borders of that collective must be reinforced to ward off those who are perceived—within this right-wing populist framework—as threats.[36]

---

34   See Fraser, "From Progressive Neoliberalism to Reactionary Populism."

35   See Fraser, Fraser, "From Progressive Neoliberalism to Reactionary Populism," 40.

36   In this context, Wendy Brown has shown why, especially in an era when national sovereignty is eroding under the pressures of globalization, border security efforts continue to intensify. See Brown, *Walled States: Waning Sovereignty*.

Achille Mbembe has offered a powerful metaphor to describe the broader context of this collective defense against fear: He speaks of the world "becoming Black." What does he mean by this? At the outset of his book *Critique of Black Reason*, Mbembe outlines three distinct phases in the relationship between exploited Black people and their White exploiters.[37] The first, spanning the fifteenth to the nineteenth century, was shaped by the transatlantic slave trade and rooted in the rise of early capitalism. During this period, it was people—largely kidnapped from West Africa—who most vividly represent Marx's insight that capitalism reduces human beings to commodities: The enslaved were quite literally turned into "human-objects, human-commodities, human-money."[38] The second phase began in the late eighteenth century and stretches to the end of the twentieth. This period was marked by a succession of struggles for freedom and civil rights—efforts to abolish slavery, decolonization movements, and campaigns against segregation and apartheid. The third phase captures the developments that Mbembe sees as underpinning his thesis of a world becoming Black. This phase begins in the late twentieth century and continues into the present day (and, one could say, beyond). According to Mbembe, it is defined by the phenomena of "the globalization of markets, the privatization of the world under the aegis of neoliberalism, and the increasing imbrication of the financial markets, the postimperial military complex, and electronic and digital technologies."[39] So in what sense can we say the world is becoming Black? Does racism not persist in our supposedly postcolonial age, more often now in a cultural rather than a biological guise? And are colonial patterns of exploitation not simply being renewed through imperialist trade systems?[40] Mbembe does not challenge such assessments at all: In fact, he sees the contemporary globalized and digitized economic

---

37   See Mbembe, *Critique of Black Reason*, 2–6.

38   Mbembe, *Critique of Black Reason*, 2.

39   Mbembe, *Critique of Black Reason*, 3.

40   See McCarthy, *Race, Empire, and the Idea of Human Development*, Chapter 3. See also Chapter 5 in the present book.

and financial order as deeply imperial in nature—still driven by "the colonial logic of occupation and extraction."[41][42]

What stands out, from his perspective, is that these systemic risks—such as being subjected to extreme exploitation, and more recently, the risk of becoming part of a "'superfluous humanity'"[43]—have now reached the urban centers of the North Atlantic world. They continue to affect racially oppressed groups most severely, but their effects are by no means limited to here. Rather, they have become "the norm for, or at least the lot of, all of subaltern humanity,"[44] whose presence is now global. In Mbembe's view, capitalism has always been racist—and still is—but today, it is also in the process of recolonizing its own core. "Never has the perspective of a Becoming Black of the world loomed more clearly. No region of the world is spared from the logics of the distribution of violence on a planetary scale, or from the vast operation under way to devalue the forces of production."[45]

This last point—the devaluation of the productive forces—makes especially clear the connection back to forms of collective identity that define themselves by excluding the Other. When right-wing populists turn to such identity formations in the form of nationalist, anti-immigration, and racist narratives, they seem—at least from my perspective—to be tapping into a collective desire to fend off the very fear triggered by the lived effects of what Mbembe describes as the universalization of the *conditio nigra*.

This makes it equally clear that right-wing populist strategies of fear do not just rely on dehumanizing tropes; they also miss the point entirely. It is not excluded Others who pose the real danger. Rather, it is the globalized risks of exploitation, precarity, and disposabil-

---

41   Mbembe, *Critique of Black Reason*, 4.

42   Empirically, these kinds of practices become especially visible in the form of land grabbing and the mass displacements that it brings. See Prien, "Kosmopolitismus und Gewalt."

43   Mbembe, *Critique of Black Reason*, 3.

44   Mbembe, *Critique of Black Reason*, 4.

45   Mbembe, *Critique of Black Reason*, 179.

ity—outgrowths of a neoliberal, unrestrained capitalism[46]—that are to blame. Right-wing populist movements and parties have not only failed to address these problems—they actively obscure them through racist and anti-immigration fear tactics.

---

46   See Žižek, *Against the Double Blackmail: Refugees, Terror, and Other Trouble with Neighbors.*

Postscript: Revisiting the Connection Between Theory and Practice?

The relationship between theory and practice has been widely debated in critical traditions of practical philosophy, social theory, and political theory throughout the twentieth century and into the present. Its definition is not straightforward for many reasons. Adorno once proposed that theory itself should be understood as a form of practice.[1] This suggestion can be read as a vision of theory grounded in radical democracy, since defining theory as practice can also be taken to mean that theory comes down from its pedestal, engages with the uncertainties of lived experience and action, and gives up the claim to predefine what practice is merely supposed to follow. In the political context of the student movement's emphatic calls for practical action, however, Adorno's statement was hardly received this way. Adorno had an ambivalent relationship with the student movement: He intellectually inspired it through his work in critical theory, but he was also uneasy with its spontaneous, often confrontational forms of activism, some of which he saw as unruly or even as mob behavior. When students occupied the Frankfurt Institute for Social Research, he even requested police protection,[2] while students waited in vain for clear professions of solidarity. Within this historical context, his comment on theory as practice could easily be understood as a refusal to support or join in those forms of political action. Across the Rhine, by contrast,

---

1   See Adorno, "Marginalia to Theory and Praxis."
2   On Adorno's ambivalent relationship to the student movement, see Stefan Müller-Dohm, *Adorno*, Part 4, Chapter 4.

Foucault—who was not initially embraced by the French political left in the 1960s—would, by the mid-1970s, propose that his theoretical work be understood as a "toolbox" for revolt.[3] Even earlier, he had expressed solidarity with students barricading themselves against police raids in Vincennes, and in the years that followed, he joined numerous demonstrations and protest marches as a political activist.[4] Here, theory is not simply put into practice; the theorist himself enters the fray of real-world struggles and confrontations.

Recalling this context—where the theory–practice relationship was fiercely debated—offers only limited guidance today. That is not only because of lingering uncertainty about what conclusions we should draw from it, but also because, as noted at the start of this book, theory no longer seems to wield the same broad influence. Still, to read this as a lament for theory's lost significance would be, in my view, mistaken. That theory is no longer invested with quasi-messianic hopes of redemption is also a sign of its democratization. Today, it can be a component—though only one of many—of practices based in civil society that aim to articulate radical, yet democratic critique. And in that role, it remains far from powerless, as we see in the attention still given to theoretical and theoretically inspired texts by politically engaged publics. Theory's impact is unpredictable and its reception often surprising: It may gain traction early on, as with Édouard Louis[5] or Geoffrey de Lagasnerie[6]—or as happened before them with Judith Butler.[7] It may center on narrative texts—beyond Louis's autobiographical novels, consider the sensation sparked by Didier Eribon's *Return to Reims*. Or it may come later in an author's intellectual development and engage with more difficult theoretical writings, as in the cases of Giorgio Agamben or Jacques Rancière. Rancière, in fact, wrote in the preface to his book *Disagreement*—which made him a major voice in contemporary political thought—that he aimed "to think

---

3   See Foucault, "Des supplices aux cellules," 1588.
4   On Foucault's political activism, see Eribon, *Michel Foucault*, part III.
5   See Louis, *The End of Eddy* and *Who Killed My Father*.
6   See de Lagasnerie, *The Art of Revolt*.
7   See Judith Butler, *Gender Trouble*.

through the effect of the return of 'political philosophy' in the field of political practice."[8]

The core argument of the present book, in any case, is that political theory should be understood as part of a critical practice—one that subjects existing realities to relentless interrogation without committing itself to constructive solutions. At present, the direction in which our societies are headed remains troublingly unclear. One need not share the optimism found in the diagnoses of Chantal Mouffe or Nancy Fraser discussed above (see Chapter 4), who detect in the wreckage of neoliberal discourse early signs of a revived left-wing politics. Just as plausibly, neoliberalism could maintain its hegemonic grip; we could enter a new phase of authoritarian populism; or—perhaps more likely—authoritarian populism could become the very form in which neoliberalism survives, albeit fractured and shot through with tension. In addition, political and social trajectories can be abruptly shaped by unforeseen events. The coronavirus pandemic, a few years ago, was one such moment, which also revealed how difficult it is to predict the medium- and long-term consequences of such crises, along with the social and political responses they provoke. Populist movements initially lost momentum, as a newfound seriousness set in under the weight of the pandemic. But at the same time, protest movements began to take shape—movements composed of an unsettling mix of far-right extremists, antiscience and antivaccine voices, and, apparently, some (former) leftists. In the medium term, their deep distrust of mainstream parties and institutions seems to be fueling the rise of right-wing authoritarian positions. A similar pattern can be observed in response to the war of aggression Russia launched against Ukraine—an event that, while not wholly unexpected, was still shocking in the sheer scale and violence of its breach of international law. On one hand, an unexpected solidarity emerged among Western democracies. But on the other, the authoritarian right seized the moment, co-opting the language of peace and gaining ground in many places.

---

8   Jacques Rancière, *Disagreement*, 17.

Still, we are not powerless in the face of these future developments, even if we cannot fully anticipate their course. It remains possible to shape and influence them. Contributing to that task, in my view, is the purpose of a critical political theory that understands itself as part of a radical-democratic practice.

This does not definitively determine the relationship between theory and practice, which may take different forms, just as the practical effectiveness of theoretical reflection remains uncertain. Nevertheless, the inquiries pursued in this essay—across various attempts to critically interrogate the present—shed light on the approximate contours of how such a critical political theory understands the nature of theory. The kind of theory proposed here does not tell us how to design a just society. It is marked by a deep skepticism toward claims of knowledge, certainty, and absolute truths. It does not ground any norms or principles. Rather, it examines how truths and norms come to be embedded in the social and political world. It does so by critically engaging with existing orders of meaning and normativity, questioning them and recognizing them fundamentally as orders of power. It neither abstracts from these structures, as normative analytic philosophy tends to do, nor does it claim to describe them objectively and neutrally, as the scientistic mainstream of empirical social science often does. Instead, it sees these arrangements as contingent institutionalizations of social and political worlds—worlds that always exist in the plural, since politics is at root a struggle over how the world is to be shaped and fundamentally possible only because no sociopolitical order rests on an unshakable foundation. One of the central tasks of a political theory that aims for critical interrogation is to keep this in view. For such a radical-democratic theory of the political, dissent and conflict are indispensable, not because the political must be grounded in conflict, but because such theory acknowledges their productive role without committing to a conflict-based ontology. This posture of interrogation may appear modest to some, but in the ongoing struggles over political transformation, it repeatedly proves to be a vital resource for emancipatory critique—one that does not shy away from interrogating even its own essentialisms.

Bibliography

Abizadeh, Arash. "Democratic Theory and Border Coercion: No Right to Unilaterally Control Your Own Borders." *Political Theory* 36, no. 1 (2008): 37–65.

Adorno, Theodor W. "Critique." In *Critical Models: Interventions and Catchwords*, translated by Henry W. Pickford, 281–288. Columbia University Press, 1998.

Adorno, Theodor W. "Marginalia to Theory and Praxis." In *Critical Models: Interventions and Catchwords*, translated by Henry W. Pickford, 259–278. Columbia University Press, 1998.

Adorno, Theodor W. *Problems of Moral Philosophy*. Edited by Thomas Schröder. Translated by Rodney Livingstone. Stanford University Press, 2000.

Allen, Amy. *The End of Progress: Decolonizing the Normative Foundations of Critical Theory*. Columbia University Press, 2016.

Arendt, Hannah. *On Revolution*. Translated by Hugh Lawson. Viking Press, 1963.

Arendt, Hannah. *The Promise of Politics*. Edited and with an introduction by Jerome Kohn. Schocken Books, 2005.

Aristotle. *Politics*. Translated by Ernest Barker and revised with introduction and notes by R. F. Stalley. Oxford University Press, 2009.

Bedorf, Thomas and Kurt Röttgers, eds. *Das Politische und die Politik*. Suhrkamp, 2010.

Benjamin, Walter. "On the Concept of History." In *Selected Writings*, vol. 4., edited by Howard Eiland and Michael W. Jennings, translated by Edmund Jephcott et al., 389–400. Belknap Press of Harvard University Press, 2003.

Blühdorn, Ingolfur. *Simulative Demokratie*. Suhrkamp, 2013.

Boghossian, Paul. *Fear of Knowledge: Against Relativism and Constructivism*. Oxford University Press, 2006.

Breckman, Warren. *Adventures of the Symbolic: Post-Marxism and Radical Democracy*. Columbia University Press, 2016.

Bröckling, Ulrich and Robert Feustel, eds. *Das Politische denken*. Transcript, 2012.

Brown, Wendy. "Neoliberalism's Frankenstein: Authoritarian Freedom in Twenty-First Century 'Democracies.'" *Critical Times* 1, no. 1 (2018): 60–79.

Brown, Wendy. *Undoing the Demos: Neoliberalism's Stealth Revolution*. Zone Books, 2015.

Brown, Wendy. *Walled States, Waning Sovereignty*. Zone Books, 2010.

Butler, Judith and Sabine Hark. "Die Verleumdung." *Zeit Online* 32, 2017. Last updated 3 August 2017. www.zeit.de/2017/32/gender-studies-feminismus-emma-beissreflex.

Butler, Judith. "Bodies in Alliance and the Politics of the Street." In *Notes Toward a Performative Theory of Assembly*, 66–98. Harvard University Press, 2018.

Butler, Judith. "Gender Politics and the Right to Appear." In *Notes Toward a Performative Theory of Assembly*, 24–65. Harvard University Press, 2018.

Butler, Judith. "We the People—Thoughts on Freedom of Assembly." In *Notes Toward a Performative Theory of Assembly*, 154–192. Harvard University Press, 2018.

Butler, Judith. *Excitable Speech: A Politics of the Performative*. Routledge, 1997.

Butler, Judith. *Frames of War: When Is Life Grievable?* Verso, 2009.

Butler, Judith. *Gender Trouble*. Routledge, 1999.

Butler, Judith. *Notes Toward a Performative Theory of Assembly*. Harvard University Press, 2018 (originally 2015).

Butler, Judith. *Precarious Life: The Powers of Mourning and Violence*. Verso, 2004.

Carens, Joseph H. "Aliens and Citizens: The Case for Open Borders." *The Review of Politics* 49, no. 2 (1987): 251–273.

Celikates, Robin. "Weder gerecht noch realistisch – David Millers Plädoyer für das staatliche Recht auf Ausschluss." Last updated

4 December 2017. http://www.theorieblog.de/index.php/2017/1
2/lesenotiz-weder-gerecht-noch-realistisch-david-millers-plae
doyer-fuer-das-staatliche-recht-auf-ausschluss/.

Crouch, Colin. *Post-democracy*. Polity, 2004.

Derrida, Jacques. "The University Without Condition." In *Without Alibi*, translated by Peggy Kamuf, 202–237. Stanford University Press, 2002.

Derrida, Jacques. "Tympan." In *Margins of Philosophy*, translated by Alan Bass, ix–xxix. University of Chicago Press, 1982.

Derrida, Jacques. *Monolingualism of the Other; or, The Prosthesis of Origin*. Translated by Patrick Mensah. Stanford University Press, 1998.

Derrida, Jacques. *Rogues: Two Essays on Reason*. Translated by Pascale-Anne Brault and Michael Naas. Stanford University Press, 2005.

Derrida, Jacques. *The Politics of Friendship*. Translated by George Collins. Verso, 1997.

Eribon, Didier. *Michel Foucault*. Translated by Betsy Wing. Harvard University Press, 1991.

Eribon, Didier. *Returning to Reims*. Translated by Michael Lucey. MIT Press, 2013.

Felsch, Phillip. *The Summer of Theory: History of a Rebellion, 1960–1990*. Translated by Tony Crawford. Polity 2021.

Flügel, Oliver, Reinhard Heil, and Andreas Hetzel, eds. *Die Rückkehr des Politischen*. Wissenschaftliche Buchgesellschaft, 2004.

Flügel-Martinsen, Oliver and Franziska Martinsen. "Ungerechtig-keit," in *Handbuch Gerechtigkeit*, edited by Anna Goppel, Corinna Mieth, and Christian Neuhäuser, 53–59. J.B. Metzler, 2016.

Flügel-Martinsen, Oliver, *Befragungen des Politischen: Subjektkonstitu-tion – Gesellschaftsordnung – radikale Demokratie*. Springer Fachmedien, 2017.

Flügel-Martinsen, Oliver. "Befragung, negative Kritik, Kontingenz: Konturen einer kritischen Theorie des Politischen." In *Kritische Theorie der Politik*, edited by Ulf Bohmann and Paul Sörensen, 450–469. Suhrkamp, 2019.

Flügel-Martinsen, Oliver. "Die Normativitätsbegründungsfalle: Die unterschätzte Bedeutung befragender und negativer Kritik-formen in der Politischen Theorie und der Internationalen

Politischen Theorie." *Zeitschrift für Politische Theorie* 2 (2015): 189–206.

Flügel-Martinsen, Oliver. "Fehlt Marx eine Theorie des Politischen?" In *"Kritik im Handgemenge": Die Marx'sche Gesellschaftskritik als politischer Einsatz*, edited by Matthias Bohlender, Anna-Sophie Schönfelder, and Matthias Spekker, 245–264. Transcript, 2018.

Flügel-Martinsen, Oliver. "Kritik." In *Radikale Demokratietheorie: Ein Handbuch*, edited by Dagmar Comtesse et al., 576–582. Suhrkamp, 2020.

Flügel-Martinsen, Oliver. "Macht zwischen Unterwerfung und Widerstand." In *Gouvernementalität, Staat und Weltgesellschaft: Studien zum Regieren im Anschluss an Foucault*, edited by Andreas Vasilache, 43–58. Springer VS, 2014.

Flügel-Martinsen, Oliver. "Negative Kritik." In *Handbuch Kritische Theorie*, vol. 1, edited by Uwe Bittlingmayer, Alex Demirovic, and Tatjana Freytag, 701–716. Springer VS, 2019.

Flügel-Martinsen, Oliver. "Postidentitäre Demokratie." *Mittelweg 36*, no. 3 (2018): 10–30.

Flügel-Martinsen, Oliver. "Sind politische Grenzen eine moralische Frage?" *Zeitschrift für philosophische Literatur* 2 (2017): 33–38.

Flügel-Martinsen, Oliver. "Subjektivation: Zwischen Unterwerfung und Handlungsmacht." In *Variationen der Macht*, edited by André Brodocz and Stefanie Hammer, 95–109. Nomos, 2013.

Flügel-Martinsen, Oliver. "Zeit der Pandemie, Zeit der harten Wissenschaft? Über einen fatalen Fehlschluss und die Perspektiven einer kritischen politischen Theorie der Pandemie," in *Kritik in der Krise: Perspektiven der Politischen Theorie auf die Corona-Pandemie*, edited by Clara Arnold, Oliver Flügel-Martinsen, Samia Mohammed, and Andreas Vasilache (Baden-Baden: Nomos 2020), 183–196.

Flügel-Martinsen, Oliver. *Radikale Demokratietheorien zur Einführung*. Junius Verlag, 2020.

Foucault, Michel, "Des supplices aux cellules." In Foucault, *Dits et Écrits*, vol. 1., 1584–1588. Gallimard, 2001.

Foucault, Michel. "Nietzsche, Genealogy, History," in *Language, Counter-Memory, Practice: Selected Essays and Interviews*. Edited by

Donald F. Bouchard. Translated by Donald F. Bouchard and Sherry Simon. Cornell University Press, 1977, 139–164.

Foucault, Michel. "The Subject and Power," in *Critical Inquiry* 8, no. 4 (1982): 777–795.

Foucault, Michel. "What Is Critique?" Translated by Kevin Paul Geiman. In *What Is Englightenment? Eighteenth-Century Answers and Twentieth-Century Questions*, edited by James Schmidt. University of Chicago Press, 1997.

Foucault, Michel. "What is Enlightenment?" In *The Foucault Reader*, edited by Paul Rabinow. Pantheon Books, 1984. Originally "Qu'est-ce que les lumières?" In Foucault, *Dits et Écrits II*, 1381–1397. Gallimard, 2001.

Foucault, Michel. *The Archaeology of Knowledge*. Translated by A.M. Sheridan Smith. Tavistock, 1972.

Foucault, Michel. *The Birth of Biopolitics: Lectures at the Collège de France 1978–1979*. Translated by Graham Burchell. Palgrave Macmillan, 2008.

Foucault, Michel. *The Order of Discourse*. Translated by Ian McLeod. Routledge, 1981.

Foucault, Michel. *The Use of Pleasure: The History of Sexuality, Volume 2*. Translated by Robert Hurley. Pantheon Books, 1985.

Fraser, Nancy. "From Progressive Neoliberalism to Reactionary Populism." In *The Great Regression: International Perspectives on the Intellectual Crisis of Our Time*, edited by Heinrich Geiselberger, translated by E. Jones, 40–49. Polity, 2017.

Friedman, Milton. *Capitalism and Freedom*. University of Chicago Press, 1962.

Fritzsche, Karl-Peter, *Menschenrechte*. Ferdinand Schöningh, 2004.

Geuss, Raymond. "Must Criticism be Constructive?" In Raymond Geuss, *A World Without Why*, 68–90. Princeton University Press, 2014.

Geuss, Raymond. *Philosophy and Real Politics*. Princeton University Press, 2008.

Gouges, Olympe de. "Les Droits de la Femme." In Olympe de Gouges, *Écrits politiques 1788–1791. Volume I*. côté-femmes, 2015.

Gouges, Olympe de. "The Declaration of the Rights of Woman (September 1791)." Translated by Lynn Hunt. https://revolution. chnm.org/d/293/.

Gramsci, Antonio. *Prison Notebooks*. Edited and translated by Joseph A. Buttigieg. Columbia University Press, 1992–2007.

Habermas, Jürgen. "Technology and Science as Ideology." In *Toward a Rational Society: Student Protest, Science, and Politics*, translated by Jeremy J. Shapiro, 81–122. Polity 2014.

Habermas, Jürgen. *Truth and Justification*. Translated by Barbara Fultner. MIT Press, 2003.

Hall, Stuart. "The West and the Rest: Discourse and Power." In *Formations of Modernity*, edited by Stuart Hall and Bram Gieben, 275–320. Polity, 1992.

Hampe, Michael. "Katerstimmung bei den pubertären Theoretikern." *Zeit Online* 52, 2016. Last updated 15 December 2016. www.zeit.de/2016/52/kulturwissenschaft-theorie-die-link e-donald-trump-postfaktisch-rechtspopulismus.

Hark, Sabine and Paula-Irene Villa. The Future of Difference: Beyond Toxic Entanglement of Racism, Sexism, and Feminism. Verso, 2020.

Hayek, Friedrich. *The Constitution of Liberty*. University of Chicago Press, 1960.

Heerich, Thomas. "Jacques Rancière: Das Unvernehmen: Philosophie und Politik." www.deutschlandfunk.de/jaques-ranciere-das-un vernehmen-politik-und-philosophie.730.de.html?dram:article_ id=101968.

Hegel, G. W. F. *Elements of the Philosophy of Right*. Translated by H.B. Nisbet. Cambridge University Press, 1991.

Hegel, G. W. F. *The Science of Logic*. Translated by George di Giovanni. Cambridge University Press, 2010.

Hegel, Georg Wilhelm Friedrich. *Lectures on the Philosophy of History*. Translated by J. Sibree, Dover Publications, 2004.

Herder, Johann Gottfried. *Ideas for the Philosophy of History of Human-ity*. Translated by T. Churchill. University of Chicago Press, 1968.

Hoare, Quintin and George Nowell Smith, eds., *Selections from the Prison Notebooks of Antonio Gramsci*. Edited and translated by Quintin Hoare and George Nowell Smith. International Publishers, 1980

Honneth, Axel. *Freedom's Right: The Social Foundations of Democratic Life*, Columbia University Press, 2014

Kant, Immanuel. "On the Different Races of Men." In *Anthropology, History, and Education*, edited by Günter Zöller and Robert B. Louden, 82–97. Cambridge University Press, 2007.

Laclau, Ernesto and Chantal Mouffe. *Hegemony and Socialist Strategy*. Verso Books, 1985.

Laclau, Ernesto. *Emancipation(s)*. Verso, 2007.

Lagasnerie, Geoffrey de. *The Art of Revolt*. Translated by Lara Vergnaud. Stanford University Press, 2023.

Lefort, Claude. "Démocratie et avènement d'un 'lieu vide.'" In *Le temps présent: Écrits 1945–2005*. 461–469. Belin, 2007.

Lefort, Claude. "La dissolution des repères et l'enjeu démocratique." In *Le temps présent: Écrits 1945–2005*, 551–568. Belin, 2007.

Lefort, Claude. "Reversibility: Political Freedom and the Freedom of the Individual." In *Democracy and Political Theory*, translated by David Macey, 165–182. Polity, 1988.

Lefort, Claude. "The Permancence of the Theologico-Political." In *Democracy and Political Theory*, translated by David Macey, 213–255. Polity, 1988.

Lefort, Claude. "The Question of Democracy." In *Democracy and Political Theory*, translated by David Macey, 9–20. Polity, 1988.

Lefort, Claude. "Vorwort zu Eléments d'une critique de la bureaucratie." In *Autonome Gesellschaft und libertäre Demokratie*, edited by Ulrich Rödl, 30–53. Suhrkamp, 1990.

Lefort, Claude. *Democracy and Political Theory*. Translated by David Macey. Polity, 1988.

Louis, Édouard. *The End of Eddy*. Translated by Michael Lucey. Farrar, Straus and Giroux, 2017.

Louis, Édouard. *Who Killed My Father*. Translated by Lorin Stein. Farrar, Straus and Giroux, 2019.

Marchart, Oliver. *Post-Foundational Political Thought: Political Difference in Nancy, Badiou, Lefort, and Laclau*. Edinburgh University Press, 2007.

Martinsen, Franziska. "Politik und Politisches." In *Radikale Demokratietheorie: Ein Handbuch*, edited by Dagmar Comtesse et al., 583–592. Suhrkamp, 2020.

Martinsen, Franziska. *Grenzen der Menschenrechte*. Transcript, 2019.

Marx, Karl. "A Contribution to the Critique of Hegel's Philosophy of Right: Introduction." In *Karl Marx: Early Writings*, translated by Rodney Livingstone and Gregor Benton, 243–258. Penguin Classics, 1992.

Marx, Karl. "Concerning Feuerbach." In *Early Writings*, translated by Rodney Livingstone and Gregor Benton, 421–423. Penguin Classics, 1992.

Marx, Karl. *Capital: A Critique of Political Economy*. Volume I. Translated by Ben Fowkes. Penguin Classics, 1976

Marx, Karl. *Capital: A Critique of Political Economy*. Volume III. Translated by David Fernbach. Penguin Classics, 1981.

Mau, Steffen. *Ungleich vereint*. Suhrkamp, 2024.

Mbembe, Achille. *Critique of Black Reason*. Translated by Laurent Dubois. Duke University Press, 2017.

McCarthy, Thomas. *Race, Empire, and the Idea of Human Development*. Cambridge University Press, 2009

Miller, David. "Reasonable Partiality Toward Compatriots." In *Ethical Theory and Moral Practice* 8 (2005): 63–81.

Miller, David. *Strangers in Our Midst: The Political Philosophy of Immigration*. Harvard University Press, 2016.

Mouffe, Chantal. *Agonistics: Thinking the World Politically*. Verso, 2013.

Mouffe, Chantal. *For a Left Populism*. Verso, 2018.

Mouffe, Chantal. *On the Political*. Routledge, 2005.

Mouffe, Chantal. *The Democratic Paradox*. Verso, 2000.

Mouffe, Chantal. *The Return of the Political*. Verso, 1993.

Müller, Jan Werner. *What is Populism?* University of Pennsylvania Press, 2016.

Müller-Dohm, Stefan. *Adorno*. Suhrkamp, 2003.

Münch, Richard. *Academic Capitalism: Universities in the Global Struggle for Excellence*. Routledge, 2014.

Nachtwey, Oliver. "Decivilization: On Regressive Tendencies in Western Societies." In *The Great Regression*, edited by Heinrch Geiselberger, 130–142. Polity, 2017.

Nachtwey, Oliver. *Germany's Hidden Crisis: Social Decline in the Heart of Europe*. Translated by Loren Balhorn and David Fernbach. Verso, 2018.

Nietzsche, Friedrich. *The Gay Science*. Translated by Walter Kaufmann, Vintage, 1974.

Oppelt, Martin. *Gefährliche Freiheit: Rousseau, Lefort und die Ursprünge der radikalen Demokratie*. Nomos, 2017.

Plato. *Complete Works*. Edited by John M. Cooper. Hackett Publishing, 1997.

Prien, Thore. "Kosmopolitismus und Gewalt: Fragen an die Weltinnenpolitik mit Blick auf Vertreibung, Landgrabbing und die Kämpfe der Subalternen." In *Gewaltbefragungen: Beiträge zur Theorie von Politik und Gewalt*, edited by Franziska Martinsen and Oliver Flügel-Martinsen, 165–183. Transcript, 2014.

Rancière, Jacques. "Politics, Identification, and Subjectivization." *October* 61, no. 61 (1992): 58–64.

Rancière, Jacques. "Who Is the Subject of the Rights of Man?" *South Atlantic Quarterly* 103, no. 2/3 (2004): 297–310.

Rancière, Jacques. *Disagreement: Politics and Philosophy*. Translated by Julie Rose, University of Minnesota Press, 1999.

Rancière, Jacques. *Hatred of Democracy*. Translated by Steve Corcoran. Verso, 2007.

Rancière, Jacques. *Modern Times: Temporality in Art and Politics*. Translated by Gregory Elliott. Verso, 2022.

Rancière, Jacques. *The Politics of Aesthetics*. Translated by Gabriel Rockhill, Continuum, 2004.

Raulff, Ulrich. *Wiedersehen mit den Siebzigern*. Klett-Cotta, 2014.

Rawls, John. *A Theory of Justice*. Harvard University Press, 1971.

Rawls, John. *The Law of Peoples*. Harvard University Press, 1999.

Redecker, Eva von. *Revolution for Life*. Translated by Charlotte Collins, Verso Books, 2023.

Said, Edward. *Orientalism*. Pantheon Books, 1978.

Sander, Lalon and Anna Böcker. "Titel der Schande." *taz*. First published 9 January 2016. www.taz.de/!5267901/.

Schwarzer, Alice. "Der Rufmord." *Zeit Online* 33, 2017. Last updated 11 August 2017. www.zeit.de/2017/33/gender-studies-judith-butler-emma-rassismus.

Soldt, Rüdiger. "Wen die 'Querdenker' wählen – und wer sie sind." *FAZ*. First published on 4 December 2020. www.faz.net/aktuell/ politik/inland/studie-zu-corona-protesten-wen-die-querdenke r-waehlen-17085343.html.

Spivak, Gayatri Chakravorty. "Can the Subaltern Speak?" In *Marxism and the Interpretation of Culture*, edited by Cary Nelson and Lawrence Grossberg, 271–313. University of Illinois Press, 1988.

Tully, James. "Anerkennung und Dialog." In Jame Tully, *Politische Philosophie als kritische Praxis*, 79–106. Campus Verlag, 2009.

Tully, James. "Public Philosophy as a Critical Activity." In *Public Philosophy in a New Key, vol. I: Democracy and Civic Freedom*, 15–38. Cambridge University Press, 2008.

Tully, James. "The Unfreedom of the Moderns in Comparison to Their Ideals of Constitutional Democracy." In *Public Philosophy in a New Key, vol. II: Imperialism and Civic Freedom*, 91–124. Cambridge University Press, 2008.

Veyne, Paul. *Foucault: His Thought, His Character*. Translated by Janet Lloyd, Polity, 2010.

Weissenburger, Peter. "Deutschland postcolognial." *taz*. First published 30 December 2016. www.taz.de/!5369967/.

Welzer, Harald. "Die Rückkehr der Menschenfeindlichkeit." *Zeit Online* 23, 2018. Last updated 29 May 2018. www.zeit.de/2018/23 /rechtspopulismus-rechtsruck-afd-migration-konsensverschie bung.

Young, Iris Marion. "Responsibility, Social Connection, and Global Justice." In *Global Challenges: War, Self-Determination and Responsibility for Justice*, 159–187. Polity 2007.

Young, Iris Marion. *Global Challenges: War, Self-Determination and Responsibility for Justice*. Polity 2007.

Young, Iris Marion. *Justice and the Politics of Difference*. Princeton University Press, 1990.

Žižek, Slavoj. *Against the Double Blackmail: Refugees, Terror, and Other Trouble with Neighbors*. Allen Lane, 2016.

Žižek, Slavoj. *The Ticklish Subject: The Absent Centre of Political Ontology*. Verso, 2009.

GPSR Authorized Representative: Easy Access System Europe, Mustamäe tee 50, 10621 Tallinn, Estonia, gpsr.requests@easproject.com

www.ingramcontent.com/pod-product-compliance
Lightning Source LLC
Chambersburg PA
CBHW070124030426
42335CB00016B/2258